real estate

listing magic

Other Books By Gael Himmah

THE LISTING MASTER

REAL ESTATE SELLING MAGIC

THE GAEL HIMMAH SYSTEM FOR INCREASING REAL
ESTATE SALES (Extensively revised September, 1974 and re-published as REAL ESTATE SELLING MAGIC)

GAEL HIMMAH PUBLISHING COMPANY
P.O. Box 4591
Walnut Creek, Calif. 94596

⊕ **GAEL HIMMAH**

Listing Magic ⊕

Real Estate

Real Estate Listing Magic
by Gael Himmah

© 1964 by Gael Himmah, P.O. Box 4591
Walnut Creek, Calif. 94596

Library of Congress Catalog Card Number: 64–21752

PRINTED IN THE UNITED STATES OF AMERICA

76424—B&P

ISBN–0–9600488–0–4

REVISED 1976

Sixteenth Printing .... August, 1976

For
Bobbie and Stevie

Preface

This book explains in detail the procedures to follow to secure listings on residential properties.

Listing will earn Real Estate income more surely than any other activity. Eighty percent of the dollars produced in the general brokerage business can be directly related to listing activity.

Residential property is our target, for single family dwellings constitute the backbone of the general brokerage business. More Real Estate sales people are engaged in the selling of homes than in all other phases of the industry combined.

Although there have been scores of books written on the subject of listing, I have yet to find one which tells the listing agent exactly what to do and exactly what to say when he is facing the homeowner across a coffee table.

Most Real Estate salesmen and brokers ask the same question, "Just what do I say when I talk to a prospective seller? What words do I use?"

This book is a step-by-step dissection of the professional listing technique; a face-to-face dialogue between homeowner and Real Estate lister.

I assume the reader has a fundamental knowledge of listings and their function in Real Estate. However, there is a vast store of information relating to listing which, if known by the prospective listing agent, would make his efforts much more successful.

The following pages constitute both a basic and an advanced course, affording the earnest reader finally with a post-graduate knowledge of the art and function of making money in Real Estate listings.

GAEL HIMMAH
Alamo, California

Contents

The Rewards
of Listing

1

I AM IN THE REAL
estate business to make money. If this were not a primary goal, I

would do better to choose another line of work, for professional, dollar-producing real estate requires long hours of hard work.

I shudder when I hear someone say, "I'm going to retire soon and go into real estate." What a shock that person's going to have.

The profession is too complex, too dynamic, and far too competitive to allow success to come without great effort. But therein lies the charm, the grace of real estate, for success is readily attainable by anyone who is sincerely interested in acquiring knowledge, willing to work, and motivated by ambition. Real estate rewards effort lavishly. In this regard, no other industry is its equal.

Listing Is
Creative Selling

By developing my skill as a listing specialist, I can earn large sums of money more surely and regularly than in any other pursuit. I am not dependent upon the whims and caprices of unknown buyers for my income production.

I do not have to wait for people to come to me before I can go into action as an income producer. A real estate licensee who limits his activity to selling does just this. He is a reactor—waiting to react to other people's actions.

Not I! Every day of every week I can walk out of my office and find many people who want to sell their property. I can list this property for sale. I then have an absolute monopoly on making money. Think of it. Once I have secured the listing, I am assured of realizing a certain income accrual regardless of who sells the property.

Listing
Assures Control

The real estate salesman who devotes his time exclusively to selling does not enjoy any kind of monopoly. Every other salesman in his marketing area is competing with him to sell a certain property before he can. In addition, this salesman does not have absolute control over his buying prospect. Again, any other salesman in his marketing area can contact his client and attempt to sell him a property. There is no protection from salesman competition, a major obstacle to real estate success.

But in listing, due to the monopolistic features of an exclusive right to sell listing, competition from other licensees is eliminated. If the property sells, the listing salesman is assured of profit.

A good lister is necessarily a good salesman. A good salesman is not necessarily a good lister. Listing requires a special technique, and is far more dependable as an income producer than is selling.

A listing specialist does not have to spend hours looking at scores of houses each week. He does not have to try to remember the myriad floor plans, front elevations, and kitchen arrangements of all those houses. He does not have to taxi prospective buyers all over town, escorting them through houses, hoping that one 'clicks.' He does not have to sit around the office and wait for the telephone to ring or someone to walk in the front door expressing an interest to buy a home. He does not have to play detective with a buying prospect, attempting to sleuth out the kind of house he really wants, or the amount of money he will really spend. Most buyers don't know this themselves.

The selling salesman has placed himself in a difficult position before he walks into his office each morning. The very nature of his selling functions are nebulous at best.

The listing specialist can spend all of his time in activities that lead directly to income production. The real estate listing specialist is a man of action!

Certainly a producing selling salesman is also a man of action, but the point of origin of that action is different.

A listing salesman is dependent upon himself, and no one else, for his income. Any morning he chooses, he can secure a listing. A percentage of his listings will sell. The listing specialist will be amply rewarded.

A good lister can earn $15,000 a year. He can earn $20,000 a year with greater effort. A top lister, working full time at listing, if he has drive, imagination, knowledge, and stamina, can exceed $30,000 in yearly income.

Additional Benefits of Listing

In my office, I prefer my salesmen to combine listing and selling activity. Once they become competent listers, they are forever after good income producers.

A salesman new to real estate should seriously consider developing a proficiency in listing as his first step toward achieving his individual goal. Any general brokerage salesman who is dissatisfied with his present income, regardless of his tenure in real estate, should develop his skill as a listing specialist.

Listing ability and its reward of continual income opens the door to all the facets within the real estate industry. Perhaps, after a thorough background in general brokerage, the licensee will want to work on commercial or industrial properties. With his listing knowledge, he is secure, knowing he can always earn a good living.

Many times I have talked with licensees who tell me they aren't going to fool around with the penny ante stakes of the general brokerage business. They have delusions of grandeur, speaking in wondrous tones about their future in land development, commercial development, and allied, complicated pursuits.

These are men who have not served a real estate apprenticeship. They have no background in the basics. These men, self-styled "big operators," most often have holes in their shoes and their trousers have that "blue serge shine"! Whereas the competent lister has money to spend. He has money to invest. He has plenty of time to go after the pot of gold.

Listing is the key to success in real estate. There is no doubt about that. An inexperienced salesman will gain confidence in himself by causing people to sign listing contracts. He will feel he is progressing.

A discouraged, non-producing salesman will benefit from listing. The act of motivating people is a powerful anesthetic to a bruised ego. Listing ability gives a feeling of security. It helps one identify with real estate.

All licensees should be aware of a real estate truism, so germane as to merit endorsement by successful real estate persons everywhere.

If You Don't List,
You Don't Last!

Listing is the key. The following chapters will show you how to put it in your hand.

Becoming a
Professional Lister

2

MY FIRST DAY IN
the real estate business was a sobering experience.

It was a crisp, clear, spring day in San Francisco. There wasn't a trace of fog. It appeared to be a fine day to start a new career.

I barely had time to tuck my new business cards into my shirt pocket and sit down at my desk, before the sales manager announced that he was going to show me how to list. He mumbled something about the importance of listing. I don't recall his message precisely. I only remember that within minutes we were speeding across town in his automobile.

He drove up a steep hill and braked to a stop in the middle of the block. I followed him up the front steps of a house and stood directly behind him as he pushed the doorbell.

My heart pounded with the uneasy pulse of the fledgling sales-man. Emotions, kindled by the unknown, can strike a person with feelings of total misery. I felt miserable! Regardless of the years of sales experience I had logged, this was new to me. I hadn't yet learned the answers. I couldn't even imagine the questions!

The door opened and a rather pleasant appearing lady smiled as the sales manager thrust his business card under her nose.

"I'm Frank Thurston," he announced, with apparent pride, "from Bushnell Realty." He motioned to me. "And this is my asso-ciate, Gael Himmah." I couldn't think of anything to say. I smiled at the lady.

Mr. Thurston continued, pursuing her graciousness like a tiger. "Are you thinking of selling your home?"

She smiled more sweetly than ever. "No, gentlemen," she re-plied, "I am not."

The door closed before us.

My sales manager was not the least dismayed.

"That's it, Gael," he announced triumphantly. "That's how we list. Go to it boy!"

He turned, pointed his index finger at arm's length and swept his arm across the panorama of hills jam packed with houses. They were "row" houses, stuck up against each other, sharing common walls, reminiscent of cell blocks at that distance. It was awesome.

"They're all out there, fella," he advised. "Go get 'em."

I wondered why he didn't say, "Sic 'em." It would have been

appropriate. He skipped gingerly down the steps to the sidewalk and opened the door of his car.

"Its ten-thirty now. I'll pick you up at the corner of Victoria and Arch at five sharp."

He disappeared in a cloud of smoke.

My formal training had been concluded.

A Decision
for Real Estate

How depressed I felt at that moment! I looked once again at that unbelievable mass of houses, all with ominous, closed doors.

Without hesitation I marched back down the steps, proceeded down the hill, rounded the corner and stopped at my destination, a sidewalk newspaper rack in front of a drug store. I deposited a dime and turned quickly to the "MEN WANTED" ads. I was searching for a better job opportunity. Alas, the only job that sounded remotely interesting would also require door to door canvassing. I breathed a sigh, deposited my newspaper in a waste can and started back up that hill. The die was cast.

I spent the next few hours going door to door, asking each homeowner if he was interested in selling his home. Each answer was the same—"no." I was getting along famously; no problems, no insults, just the same question and the same answer, time after time.

And then it happened!

I rang a doorbell and a man answered. I asked my question. "Would you be interested in selling your home?"

"Yes," he replied without hesitation, "I would."

"My God!" I whispered to myself. I was dumbfounded. I was totally unprepared for this unlikely occurrence.

I suddenly remembered that I didn't even have any listing forms with me. My sales manager hadn't given them the slightest thought. He must have known the value of his instruction! I decided to pursue my opportunity as best I could.

"After all," I thought to myself, fabricating confidence desperately, "I'm a state licensed real estate salesman. I probably know more than I realize." I felt better.

"I would like to ask you a question, if I might," the homeowner said. He was almost apologetic.

I adopted my most learned expression. "Yes?"

My subject continued. "My neighbor tells me if I sell my house, I'll have to pay some extra money," he hesitated, thinking, "something called 'points.'"

"Called what?" I questioned, the expression being foreign to me.

"Points," he replied.

I saw my opening, my chance to prove conclusively his need of my superior knowledge.

"That's just why you need my services," I admonished. "You shouldn't listen to those old wives' tales. I'm a licensed real estate salesman and I've never heard of such a thing—points! You can thank your lucky stars I came along!" I was feeling victorious. Someone needed me after all!

I did not get the listing. I don't remember exactly why. Perhaps his wife was not home and I would need her signature, if I had a listing contract, that is. But this is not important to this story.

When I returned to the office late that afternoon, I asked about the mysterious word I had learned from the friendly gentleman. I asked about "points."

The shock I received has never departed my conscious memory.

Points did exist, I was informed. Had I succeeded in taking the listing, had the homeowner taken my advice, he would have suffered a financial loss of $1,100. (The mechanics of points will be discussed later in detail.) I was horrified. The enormity of what I had nearly done impressed upon me my desperate need for knowledge.

If someone had only given me the information which would let me perform as a professional, I would have been spared so much future embarrassment. I would have been able to do a better job for my clients. I would have earned more money more quickly.

This incident is humorous in retrospect, but living the experience was bitter. There shall never be a substitute for preparation!

Unfortunately, the average real estate salesman entering the business doesn't receive much more help than I did. Upon receipt of his new license, he is ill-prepared to earn a living, let alone make really substantial sums of money. In order to receive his license, he had only to learn some of the theory of the business. He didn't have to learn anything about making money.

He knows how to fill in the blanks on a deposit receipt form, but he doesn't know how to get a buyer to sign it.

Most new salesmen are given a desk, a set of business cards and the telephone, and sent out to "beat the bushes," to list, or sell some houses. What a helpless feeling they have! I know! They don't know where to go or what to do. It's no wonder that many potentially valuable real estate salesmen are frightened out of the business before they've had an opportunity to test their mettle.

Specialize. Real estate today is a profession. In the classic professions—medicine, law, dentistry—specialists normally enjoy a greater income accrual than general practitioners. The same is true in real estate. Specialists make more money! Once I had entered the business, my immediate goal was making money, and making it as soon as possible.

From somewhere back in a cobwebbed cranny of my mind I remembered an old chestnut, an axiom of business success which goes something like this: "If you want to be successful, do what others find unpleasant."

I also brought to mind the maxim: "He who puts merchandise on the shelf earns greater rewards than he who merely takes it off."

I saw that very few real estate salesmen concentrated their efforts on listing. They listed only if there was nothing else to do. Listing, by my contemporaries, had been exiled to an inferior role. Without further ado, I decided to become a listing specialist.

Listing means meeting new people. This requires a certain amount of fortitude. That, in itself, would eliminate as competition a large percentage of the other real estate salesmen. They have found it all too easy to equate moderate success with contentment.

How fortunate my decision! Since that first trauma-filled day, I have never realized less than $1,000 income per month from my listing activities, even when I listed only several hours per week. When I listed full time, my income swelled rapidly to an astounding sum.

Put Goods on the Shelf. The significance of listing in general brokerage is obvious. A listing is the beginning of most real estate transactions. Without a listing, the salesman cannot be certain of receiving a commission when he performs. A listing protects all co-operating salesmen.

A listing on a property is like merchandise on the shelf. The only difference is that it doesn't cost the real estate lister any money to purchase his merchandise. His only expenditure is time. A real estate broker without listings will soon find himself out of business.

Whenever I take a listing and submit it to our local multiple listing service, I immediately have 900 salesmen working for me. This armada of salesmen doesn't cost me a cent, yet they are actually in competition with each other, vying to see which one can bring me an acceptable sales contract first.

To express it differently, all of these salesmen are working as diligently as they can to put money in my pocket. It's like owning a giant corporation, with a huge sales force which works for nothing, the merchandise is free, and the income is all for me. Think of it. There's nothing like it anywhere in business. What a fantastic opportunity!

Of the scores of books written on real estate, there is one premise on which practically all authors agree: a good lister will make at least as much, and usually more, money than a good salesman. Moreover, there is much less competition in listing.

Listing Is Easy. At listing seminars, I am often asked if listing isn't much more difficult than selling. To most salesmen this seems to be true. But it isn't. Listing is really much easier than selling and much, much more rewarding.

I believe it is fair to equate listing, by a professional lister, to a game of chess. Sellers who attempt to sell their homes themselves have only a few stock reasons as to why they don't want to sign a listing contract. I believe I have heard every objection. I have also had time to create and test logical, believable answers to each of these objections.

When a professional lister begins talking to a "For Sale by Owner," he knows in advance the objections the seller will use as a defense. He also has his time-proven answers ready. It is really no contest. It is unfair competition.

How I would like to know in advance all my opponent's moves, and all my moves and countermoves, when I play chess. I would be the all-time world master without doubt.

In chess it will never happen, but in listing, where you can line your pockets with silver, it not only can, but will happen if you study carefully the information on the pages of this book. You will soon find yourself able to master any situation that arises within the province of listing.

Listing Causes Income. Real estate selling is reactive selling. You must wait for the prospective buyer to come to you. Listing, however, is creative selling in its purest form. A lister does not wait for someone to show interest first, as in selling. He creates the interest himself.

Every so often I meet a real estate broker who feels listings aren't the principal vehicles on the road to fiscal Utopia. I can seldom resist drawing these persons into a discussion to determine the logic behind their opinion.

Invariably, the cardinal reason for such a feeling is the same among them all. They rationalize their lack of aggressiveness, their daily modus operandi as reactors instead of originators, to such an extent that they truly believe they are functioning at peak performance.

If a salesman is satisfied with his income production, he will usually remain static in his development as an income producer rather than suffer the agonizing growing pains of new sales experiences. Hence, rationalization, that omnipotent balm of the reactor-type salesman, spreads itself soothingly across the conscience and presto, "listing isn't important!"

If a salesman was to depend on his income from sales to pay his regular monthly expenses, he would be walking a treacherous path. Listing income should pay the bills.

Listing Income Should Pay Expenses. I recommend that a new real estate salesman, upon entering the business, carefully determine the amount of money he will require to meet his regular monthly living expenses and obligations.

He should make up his mind to earn the money to meet these obligations from listing income. The creative sales aspect of listing seems to dictate this to any prudent person. When a real estate salesman lists, he is forced to sell, since many home owners will want to buy another home in the same locality after their present home is sold. Hence, sales income, which we agree is reactive type income, should be considered the "gravy" of the real estate business.

Since sales income is dependent in large measure on the vagaries of buyers' fancies, the amount of sales income to be earned in any given month cannot be accurately forecast. Listing income can be predicted wtih uncanny precision.

In the marketing area where I conduct my real estate business, we calculate that the average listing commission paid to a salesman is $500. The average selling commission paid to a salesman is $1,000. It is readily evident that a sale puts twice as much money in the agent's pocket as a listing sold. This is the point at which most real estate salesmen halt their processes of reasoning.

We further calculate that at least one listing out of every three will sell. If a salesman has to make at least $1,000 per month to meet his expenses, he should secure six new listings every month.

After he has secured six listings, the new salesman can spend his time selling. He will be a better salesman because he won't be worrying about paying his bills. His monthly listing activity will become mechanical, in a sense. He knows he must bring in six new listings each month, so he does just that. It is not an arbitrary quota, just an expression of economic necessity, and he knows it!

This simple formula can be applied with accuracy to any given commission schedule, any sales price range, and any income requirement level.

For a salesman to sell a house, a prospective buyer has to come to him and express an interest in buying. Certainly advertisements in newspapers and realty signs on homes direct purchasers to a salesman, but the fact remains that the buyer motivates himself to look at homes in the first place.

A salesman can't grab a pedestrian off the street, haul him into his office by his collar, and sell him a home. A salesman has to wait for the buyer to come to him. Therefore, he is dependent upon the vagaries of buyers to make his money. That, doubtless, is a poor position for any salesman to be in.

Reduce Human Variables. Consider how secure the real estate agent would be if he could reverse the relative positions of salesman and customer so that his income was dependent upon his own inclinations. That's exactly what the salesman is doing when he concentrates his efforts on listing.

There are always homeowners who want to sell their homes. On the average, only one out of every 500 homeowners will sell his home without the assistance of a real estate agent. The average homeowner sells his home every seven years.

Quickly you can see the ever rich vein of listings in your own sales areas. It is the salesman's own private gold mine for just as long as he wishes. It will never "peter out." He can mine when he wants. His income will grow in direct proportion to his labors. He's the boss, completely, and his only investment is professional skill.

It's not difficult to acquire such skill. The field is wide open. There is surprisingly little competition. Don't ever forget that professional listing can pile money into one's personal bank account just as fast, and as high, as he desires.

Principles of
Successful Listing

3

BEFORE WE CAN EN-
ter into a detailed discussion of the specifics of listing, there is some

basic information which the professional lister should commit to memory. At present, this grab bag of miscellaneous information will be uncorrelated to the formula for listing which we shall ultimately develop. It will fit nicely into place as we progress.

There will be slight variations in some of the following figures dependent upon local conditions in different areas across the country; however, this information can be readily adapted to meet any such local conditions. The principles remain the same.

Listing
Time Table

An acceptable sales contract is received, as an average, on a new, single family, residential property approximately 80 days after the listing was first taken. Although sellers should be advised that the average home sells 80 days from the listing date, they should also be made aware of the fact that only one out of four homes that are on the market at any given time sell during their first term of listing.

Everyone has heard of a home going on the market in the morning and selling the same afternoon. This is highly unusual and most often occurs when the home sells for a price lower than its true fair market value, or, if the home is in perfect condition, or if it is in a location of acute demand and extremely limited supply.

The homeowner who expects his home to sell shortly after signing a listing contract is a seriously misinformed seller. It is the duty of the listing agent to explain the time mechanics of listing and sales carefully to the seller.

There seems to be a period of sales inertia after a property is first listed. You can overcome this by spreading the word about the availability of the home to other salesmen and giving information as to loan commitments and methods of financing.

Home Value
Guides

The professional lister should know the percentage figure applicable to his local market area regarding the yearly appreciation of single family dwellings. In my area, a home appreciates on the average of 9% a year. By the same token, our dollar is losing value at the approximate rate of 8% a year. This leaves the homeowner with a net gain of 1% a year from his investment in home ownership. This is money in his pocket.

A homeowner has to live in his home about 1½ years before he will break even on sales price less commission when equated to the number of dollars he spent to purchase the home. This is considering he made only normal improvements such as carpets and drapes, landscaping and maintenance.

The Story of "Points"

If we expect a homeowner to list his home with us, we must first earn his respect for us as professionals. Nothing I have ever used in my listing experiences has done more to gain that respect quickly as the following discourse on "points." Its language is professional; the story is packed with information; the progression is believable.

Most sellers have heard of "points." They've heard "points" cost them hundreds of dollars. "Points" are fleeting mavericks that sellers don't understand but speak of in frightened, angry tones. This story puts a sugar coating on a nationally bitter pill. Learn it as best you can.

A thorough knowledge of FHA-GI points is indispensable to the successful lister. You should ask the seller if he understands what points really are. If he is honest, he will confess he does not.

I agree with the seller when he objects to paying points. "I don't blame you for resenting even the mention of points, Mr. Hansen," I begin, "but there's a good reason for their existence. I've had to pay points myself, and it always seemed so unfair for the seller to have to pay money so that a buyer could get a loan.

"When I finally learned about points in detail, when I learned the history of points and what was actually behind them, I was thankful for their existence. If you have the time and the interest, I will be happy to tell you about points.

"You know, Mr. Hansen, you would be surprised how many homeowners I talk to don't want to learn about points. They understand that the absence of this knowledge could cost them hundreds upon hundreds of dollars, but they just don't want to make the effort to learn. Would you like me to tell you about points? It'll only take a few minutes."

What can a seller say after a preface like that? Certainly he's interested. If you commit the following dialogue on points to memory, adjusting the sentence structure to fit your own method of speaking, you can practically overwhelm the seller with your high level of professionalism.

Dialogue
of Points

In 1944, when Congress knew World War II would soon be over and there would be a tremendous demand for housing by the returning veterans, they passed emergency legislation known as the Servicemen's Readjustment Act of 1944.

You are familiar with some of the tenets of that Act, Mr. Hansen. The GI Bill Of Rights, which sent so many veterans to college, was part of the Act. It also provided for a veteran's farm and home purchase section whereby the federal government would guaranty, or insure, lenders against loss on a GI mortgage loan within specified limits.

When there is a huge demand for housing, and the supply of housing is limited, the price of housing goes up. Hand in hand with this, since practically all purchases of housing are dependent upon mortgage financing, the demand for, and therefore the cost of, mortgage financing increases.

The money that is made available for mortgage loans is not advanced by the government. The federal government only insures the lenders against loss. The money itself comes from private institutional lenders such as banks and insurance companies. These lenders deal in a product just like a grocer deals in bread and potatoes. Their product is money. They rent money! Their income is derived from the rental fees they charge for their money. This they call interest.

With this sudden demand for mortgage money caused by the returning veterans, a lender might first think of raising the interest rates for this money. But the government foresaw that possibility and so wrote into the Act, which became federal law, a provision which sets the statutory maximum rate of interest that can be charged by these lenders.

Now, these lenders are independent businessmen. They are in business to make a profit just like other businessmen. They have to answer to their stockholders and investors. They aren't interested in giving money away. They could not raise their interest rates above the federally specified maximum limit. They would have to look elsewhere for a way to increase their yield from dollars invested.

There are two principal sources of investment for most institutional lenders. They are limited as to their types of investment by state and federal statute. They can put their money into either the security bond market or into mortgage loans.

The security bond market is relatively stable. It has functioned at the level of 9¼% for quite some time now. This means, that for every dollar a lender invests in the bond market, he will realize a return on his investment, a yield, of 9¼%.

The federal government has set the current maximum limit a lender can charge on a GI loan at 8¾%. Mr. Veteran wants to borrow $15,000 in order to buy a home and he asks the lender, let's call him the First National Bank, to loan him the money.

First National doesn't want to make the loan since they would realize a yield of only 8¾%, whereas, if they put the same $15,000 into the bond market, they would realize a yield of 9¼%.

It looks, for the moment, as if the GI home loan program was doomed from the start. But the lenders said they would make the loans if they could take in enough cash at the time the loan was made to raise their effective rate of interest to 9¼%. The lenders wanted to charge a loan discount fee.

The government was not opposed to this. However, they kept clearly before them the premise that the purpose of the Act was to facilitate the purchase of a home, not the sale of a home. This is the essence of all government-insured financing, both GI and FHA.

Because of this, Congress said that if a premium was to be charged by a lender in order to make a loan, the purchaser could not pay it. Since there are only two parties to a sale, that left the seller.

Across the entire United States, the average mortgage loan is paid off every eight years. Institutional mortgage lenders have found this to be so.

Each percentile of a loan that a lender collects in cash at the time the loan is made will increase the lender's effective rate of interest ⅛th of 1% over the term of the loan.

As an example of this, if a lender is going to make a loan of $15,000 at 8¾% interest, and the lender can collect 2% of the principal amount of the loan in cash at the time the loan is made. $300. the lender will actually realize a yield of 9% over the term of the loan. These amounts of cash collected by lenders at the time they make mortgage loans are referred to as loan discount fees. They are more commonly called POINTS.

A point is 1% of the loan requested. If a buyer wants a $15,000 loan, one point would be $150. If the lender collected just one point, his rate of interest would increase ⅛th of 1%. If he collected two points, his rate of interest would increase ¼%, and so forth.

Since the lender can invest in the bond market, and make 9¼%, if he desires, and that same lender can earn only 8¾% interest on a GI loan, he must charge enough points to increase his yield to 9¼% if he is to make the loan to our veteran purchaser.

The difference between 8¾% and 9¼% is ½%. This is the same as ⁴/₈ths. Hence, the lender must charge the seller four points if a GI loan is to be made to the buyer.

A man buying a home under the FHA program can be considered in the same light as a veteran purchaser under the GI program as concerns points, since there are also federal statutory regulations governing the maximum rate of interest a lender can charge a FHA purchaser.

In some areas of the country, the number of points will vary dependent upon local market conditions. If personal savings are at a high level, and lenders have large sums of money they want to invest in mortgage loans, competition among the various lenders for good risk loans will become keen and they will begin "shaving" points in order to attract mortgage loans to their doors.

Another factor affecting the number of points charged is the size of the buyer's down payment. The more money he puts down on a home, the more secure the lender feels, and the more willing he is to reduce his rate of effective interest.

When Congress periodically announces they are going to lower the interest rate on FHA home loans, for example, the mortgage lenders are not concerned regarding their rates of investment yield. They will merely raise their point charges to compensate for the lower interest figure. The seller has to pay the price. In some instances this is passed along to the buyer in a higher sales price.

A Sound
Business Decision

Mr. Hansen, approximately 60% of the homes in your neighborhood are sold through government-insured financing requiring the payment of points by the seller. You are under no obligation to sell to a person buying on this type of financing.

However, if you refuse to entertain offers from government-insured purchasers, you are closing your eyes to six out of every ten people who could, and might, buy your home.

Government-insured financing is attractive to the buyer because it gives him the opportunity to buy with a relatively low down payment and, in some cases, no down payment at all.

Consider that when you pay points, you are actually buying a 150% increase in the number of potential buyers for your home. Instead of four people who could buy, you now have ten.

A manufacturer who has a product to sell and wants to increase his potential market spends many thousands of dollars in advance to pay for advertising, hoping to increase his market a few percentiles.

But you, Mr. Hansen, by agreeing to pay points, are not only increasing your potential market by 150%, but you don't have to pay out any money in advance. And the money that points cost you is usually only a few hundred dollars, a reasonable sum when you consider you are asking a buyer of your home to commit himself to a mortgage loan of thousands of dollars that will encumber his family for many years to come.

When you look at it this way, points are actually a sound business investment.

That's the story of points. Speak slowly when you repeat it, for it's complex and a bit difficult to understand if your seller is not familiar with real estate financing.

Miscellaneous Notes

One of my favorite expressions is: "If you're comfortable, you're losing money."

How true this is in the general brokerage business. It takes effort to make money. The greater the effort, the greater the amount of money. You cannot sit behind a desk and wait for your office to bring customers to you. You have to go out and get it yourself.

Acquire Knowledge. A successful lister must, at all times, conduct himself as a professional person. The cornerstone of any profession is knowledge.

Learn everything you can about real estate. Continue to learn; that is one of the blessings of real estate. A human mind can absorb real estate information like a dry sponge, but the field is so wide, the subject so vast, that a person can study forever and never know it all. A quick knowledge of his subject will give the listing specialist the self-assurance necessary to effuse a professional demeanor.

I believe the professional lister should form the habit of reading at least one newspaper daily and one news magazine weekly. Keeping posted on current events will give you the ability to converse on any subject at any time. This, to the salesman, is power!

Gentle Pressure. High pressure sales tactics are strictly unacceptable to the lister. Still, it would be well to remember that the average person wants to be guided in his thoughts. He wants to be helped to his decisions, prodded if you will. Learning to detect the fine, almost invisible, line between ethical prodding and non-professional pressure marks the measure of the successful lister.

I can bring to mind several instances when I couldn't make a decision on an expensive purchase and the salesman actually sold me the merchandise. I was ever grateful to him for being such a competent salesman because I was thoroughly pleased with my purchase after it was made. That is the job of the real estate listing specialist— TO SELL!

Pointers on Selling Dialogue. In preparing your sales dialogue, do remember that if you put your "customers" in the position of having to think, you will lose them. You must suggest the answers you want. It is painful for people to think of replies when speaking with a salesman. Certainly questions are necessary, but only if they can be answered without great thought.

When your customers ask you questions, don't give answers they expect if you can avoid it. If they can accurately anticipate your answers, they will feel they don't need your help. You must sound different from the "run of the mill" salesman. To hold people's attention, you should surprise them with what you say or how you say it. Shock them! Of course you don't want to offend anyone and that isn't necessary. We will explore methods of surprising customers with our selling presentation in later chapters.

90% Commission Listings. Here is a novel concept of listing. Often

I discover a piece of property, the highest and best use of which I am uncertain.

I recently came upon a two-acre parcel of undeveloped land which the owner wanted to sell. He had a use in mind for the proceeds of the sale and knew just how much money he wanted from his land. He suggested a "net" listing assuring him a specified sum, the balance of the sales price accruing to me.

I do not like to use net listings. Should the real estate agent sell the property for a great deal more than the property owner receives, the owner often feels he has been deceived and hard feelings result.

But I was not sure of what the property might sell for since there were many commercial uses possible. I proposed a 90% listing to the seller and he was very pleased. It works like this.

The seller wanted $20,000 for himself. I charge a 10% commission for the sale of unimproved property, so the seller agreed to pay me as a commission, 10% of the sales price for any sale up to and including $22,500, which would net the seller approximately $20,000 after he paid his closing costs. In addition, the seller agreed to pay me, as a commission, 90% of the sales price for any portion of a sales price above $22,500.

If I sold the property for $30,000, I would receive 10% of the first $22,500 of the sales price and 90% of the last $7,500.

The property owner was happy because he could gain more money than he originally wanted. As the agent, I have even more incentive to promote the sale of the property for our mutual benefit.

Figure 1 illustrates my 90% listing.

AUTHORIZATION TO SELL

Antioch............., California, ...June..6,.19......

In consideration of the services of...BONANZA..REALTY,..INC................ hereinafter called the agent, I hereby list with said agent, exclusively and irrevocably, for a period of time beginning ......June...6........., 19......... and ending ....December..31........, 19........., and grant said agent the exclusive and irrevocable right to sell within said time for...THIRTY..THOUSAND..AND..NO/100..–..–..–..– ($..30,000.00.–..–..–..–..........) Dollars, and to accept a deposit thereon, the following described property in the City..of..Concord.................County of...Contra..Costa...............State of California, to-wit:

Unimproved lot, 2 acres in size, on the Southwest Corner of Clayton Road

and Golden Gate Way, vested in the name of Joe B. Smiley and Edna B.

Smiley. Said property is zoned commercial.

The purchase price shall be payable as follows: All cash to sellers.

Seller agrees to pay the agent as commission 10% of the sales price to

a price of $22,500 and 90% of the sales price for any portion of the

sales price above $22,500.

I hereby agree to pay the agent as commission SEE ABOVE. ~~XXXXXXXX XXX XXXXX XXXX XXXXX XXXXXXX~~
whether said property is sold by said agent, or by me, or by another agent, or through some other source, or if said property
is transferred, conveyed, leased or withdrawn from sale during the time set forth herein.

If within ten days after the termination of this listing, said agent notifies me in writing personally, or by mail, that
during its life, he negotiated with persons named by him, and sale is made within one hundred eighty(180) days after the
termination of this contract to any person so named, I agree to pay the agent the commission provided for herein.

If a deposit is forfeited, one-half thereof shall go to said agent as commission and one-half to me, provided, however
the agent's share shall not exceed the amount of the above named commission.

Evidence of title to be in the form of a Policy of Title Insurance issued by the LAFAYETTE TITLE COMPANY and
paid for by the buyer.

Thirty days allowed for examination of title, following receipt of the deposit. Taxes (July 1 basis), interest, insurance,
loan trust funds (if indebtedness is being assumed) and rents to be prorated. Insurance may be cancelled. When sold as
herein provided, I will convey said property to the buyer by a grant deed, and when notified of sale I will immediately
upon request deposit with said Title Company for delivery, said deed and any other documents and instructions necessary
to complete the transaction. If objection to title is reported, I agree to take immediate steps to clear title and buyer shall
within five days after title is reported cleared by the Title Company, deposit the full purchase price in escrow.

Notice of sale hereunder may be given to me by telephone, orally, or by mail to the address given below, or by
personal service.

Time is the essence hereof. In the event of the failure of a buyer to perform any of the terms hereof, all rights
of such buyer shall immediately cease and terminate.

We hereby acknowledge receipt of a copy of this contract.

Address...........57..Durham..Street..............

...............Antioch...California..............

Telephone...229..8055...............

In consideration of the above listing, the undersigned agent agrees to use diligence in procuring a buyer.

....
.... Seller.

BONANZA..REALTY...INC.
By.......................................
                              Real Estate Agent.

Figure 1

How to
Price a Listing

4

THERE HAVE BEEN
many methods advanced and much complicated maneuvering sug-

gested by real estate educators for determining the sales price to assign any given property.

I contend that the real estate agent can earn himself much trouble on this subject. By assuming the role of profesional appraiser, attempting to predetermine the sales price of a property, he can easily mastermind himself right out of the real estate business.

Pricing does not have to be difficult. It can be handled with such skill that pricing policy can actually cement the salesman's professional relationship with the seller.

A Clumsy
Method

One of the most widely recommended methods of pricing is to ask the seller what he paid for the home and how long he has lived there. Adding a certain percentage figure for local appreciation (9% in my area), the price is supposed to "pop out of a hat!"

I have also heard capable instructors suggest that the salesman ask the seller, "What is your loan balance?" Then he is to ask, "How much did you put as a down payment on the home?" And finally, "How long have you lived here?"

Adding these figures together and considering a certain percentage for local appreciation and depreciation, the salesman should have a good idea of the fair market price of the home. This is clumsy and is not professional!

Always
Be Direct

If a doctor wants to know something about your personal history before he makes his diagnosis, he asks you. When you want an answer, ask a question! As you will see in Chapter 11, when we learn the exact words to use when dealing with the homeowner, the first question I ask the seller is, "How much are you asking?" I can then add on the commission, in my mind, and I know what the home has to sell for in order to net the seller what he wants.

List at Any Price. I depart radically from most instructors in the field of real estate sales in that I advocate taking a listing at any price. Those real estate educators who disagree are not expert listers. I earned my living for years doing nothing but listing. I know whereof I speak!

So often I hear instructors and brokers advising real estate licensees not to take a listing more than 5% or 10% or some percentile over what it will sell for. They all seem to have a percentage rule of thumb predicated on the sales price of the property. To them I direct the questions, "Just what will a given house sell for? What will an unknown buyer pay for a house he has not yet seen?"

Of course the answers are identical. No one can predict accurately what a property will sell for. It is impossible. Real estate appraising is not an exact mechanical science. It is, at best, an expression of individual appraiser's reaction to any given property, governed to some degree by a set of rules. No two appraisers will come up with identical figures.

Recognizing that homes are purchased on emotion, how can anyone suppose he can judge the emotional reaction of an unknown buyer to a given property and then equate that reaction to the buyer's own purchasing habits? Such a person would have to possess supernatural powers! Only if the home is located in a large subdivision where all the homes are nearly identical can anyone accurately predict the sales price.

Eliminate Competition. I never forget that my primary function as an income producer is to eliminate my listing competition—the other real estate salesmen in my marketing area. Once I have the listing, I am no longer concerned with them as competitors. Then I can devote my energies to getting the listing sold or the price reduced. But first, and always first, I must secure the listing.

There is a less obvious benefit from having an overpriced listing. The real estate sign displayed on the property serves as an excellent piece of institutional advertising. The more signs a realtor has displayed about a city, the better!

Pricing Dialogue. I believe in educating the seller when he asks me what his home will sell for. I tell him something like this:

Mr. Wilson, the price you put on your home will play a very important role in the success of its sale. Three things cause a home to sell: price, location, and condition.

If the location and condition are good and the terms are reasonable, the price then becomes the all important factor. Location cannot be changed. Condition can be improved. If this is done and the home still doesn't sell, price is the culprit!

You should understand, Mr. Wilson, that single family dwellings are bought and sold because of emotion. Homes are not purchased like apartment buildings, where the investor takes a long, cold, calculating look at the income and expense history of the building, leaving emotion to the luxurious haunts of home buyers.

No one can say what emotional reaction any given buyer will have to your home, and certainly no salesman could then calibrate this reaction to the purchasing habits of his unknown buyer.

I believe in giving you, the homeowner, all the information I have about similar properties, about market conditions and about financing, and then letting you set the price yourself. Recognizing how important a factor emotion is in causing a home to sell, you must help with the price for no one knows more about the emotional qualities of your home than you. I make certain that you know as much as I about relative prices of comparable homes. I'm going to give you a real estate education!

Mr. Wilson, homes can most accurately be priced by a method we in the trade call "comparative analysis." This means that we compare sales prices of homes similar to yours. You must remember that regardless of what you paid for the home, regardless of what you feel the home is worth, it will only sell for what someone is willing to pay for it. It is worth no more. Prices of comparable homes are very important.

At this point, I tell him what several comparable homes recently sold for in his neighborhood. I continue.

The most significant factors to consider in comparing homes are location, style, and square footage. Age and condition come next. Lot sizes and extra improvements also affect sales price.

Mr. Wilson, considering all of these things, I want you to tell me what you consider the best price for your home.

The seller doesn't quite know what to make of the lister. Other salesmen have either told him they can get an astounding price, which caused him to distrust them and their judgment, or else they gave him a price that was far below what he wanted. If he then gives you a price, and it seems realistic, use it. If the price is high, tell him!

> Mr. Wilson, I believe your price is high. It is not so high, however, that we will scare buyers off. You see, there is a limit above which a price will actually cause so much sales resistance that you won't even stimulate an offer. We can't exceed that limit.
> We can always come down in price, but it is next to impossible to raise a price once it is established. Of course [and say this with a grin], the more we sell your home for, the more money I make.

If the price the seller has mentioned is completely unreasonable, be sure to tell him just that. However, if he still wants to try to market his home at that price, and the agent has made him understand the probable folly of his decision, I say go ahead and take the listing.

An Example of an "Overpriced" Listing

There is an attractive subdivision several miles from my office where I have made a good deal of money over the years.

The homes are nearly identical—Brittany ranchers, three bedrooms, two baths, heavy shake roofs, and beautiful view lots. The homes are small, about 1100 square feet of living area. I have listed and sold many of these homes. They sell from $35,000 to $38,000; not more, not less.

A year ago I had a listing on one of these homes and it sold for $36,500. About nine months later, the homeowner called me to say he was being transferred to Chicago and he wanted to sell his home. Needless to say, I was delighted!

I arrived at his home that evening with a listing contract already filled out. All that was required to make it legal was his signature. I had entered the standard $36,500 price. When I showed him the listing contract he advised me that he wanted to put his home on the market at $45,000. He agreed that he had not made any major improvements in the home. He just wanted to try $45,000.

I knew that he would be leaving shortly for Chicago and figured that after he was located in his new home he would grow weary of his ridiculous price and authorize a price reduction. I also recognized the need to eliminate my competition. I knew the house would have to sell eventually, so I consented to take the listing at $45,000.

I was embarrassed when I gave the listing information to the other salesmen in my office. How they kidded me! They all knew it was grossly overpriced. I told them I was making an investment in the future, but the hazing continued unabated. These salesmen were good appraisers and good salesmen. They wouldn't even waste their time showing the property to prospective purchasers.

Five days later the listing was distributed on our multiple listing service. I was more embarrassed. I had a reputation to uphold!

But the following day, one day after the listing was published to our real estate board members, I received two telephone calls from two different brokers informing me that they each had full price offers on the property.

I was amazed. What's more, when the prospective buyers discovered someone else had made an offer, they wanted to get into a bidding contest.

My seller was thrilled. I was surprised. My salesmen were poorer because they had outsmarted themselves. True, I had made a serious error in pricing, but because I had taken a supposed overpriced listing, and because of the absolute protection a listing affords the agent, I made money despite myself!

The moral of the story is obvious. Don't mastermind yourself out of the real estate business. Experienced real estate agents are continually surprised at the "high" prices buyers pay for property and the "low" prices sellers accept.

Square Foot Appraisals

An appraisal based upon an analysis of the square footage replacement costs is very helpful in determining price. The estimated value of the lot the home is built upon is added to the replacement cost figure of the improvements. Local labor and material costs are also considered.

The primary disadvantage of this method of pricing is the time element. While one salesman is measuring, inspecting and computing, another salesman, using the pricing policy I suggest, will be getting a listing contract signed.

There is plenty of time for square-foot appraising after the listing has been taken. Urgency is the mark of a prosperous sales person. Methodical plodding distinguishes the "also rans."

Price
Economics

It would be well to understand a fundamental economic principle which bears directly on the entire subject of price. I discuss this with the homeowner. It is an interesting subject and does much to project a professional image. It also dissuades the homeowner from setting an unusually high price on his home should he feel he has something extra special to offer.

In our free, competitive economy, the single most important factor in determination of price of any article is SCARCITY. Supply, demand, and utility are the three basic catalysts of our economy. Supply and scarcity are practically the same. Demand and utility are important in establishing price, but not to such an extent as scarcity.

Consider the items, diamonds and water. Water is in great demand among the people of the world. Certainly water is a necessity of life. It's utility is prodigious. On the other hand, diamonds are not in great demand among all the peoples of the world. Diamonds have a limited functional use. But diamonds are very expensive and water is cheap. The cause is *scarcity*. Water is in abundant supply and diamonds are scarce.

Consider the dodo bird. They are extinct. There is practically no demand for them. There is not much use for a dodo bird except, perhaps, for scientific study. But if you were suddenly to come into possession of a dodo bird, alive and flapping, you would have a valuable treasure. That value could be attributed to its scarcity.

A home in the middle of a large subdivision, where many similar homes are for sale, cannot command a price higher than the other homes although there is a demand for such a home and the home has an obvious utilitarian function. The function of scarcity is not present.

A home that is unusual in design, and is so designed as to be nonfunctional and aesthetically distasteful, will be the "white elephant" of the real estate market. Someone will eventually buy it, but the price will strike mortal terror in the heart of the seller. Scarcity is the fulcrum of price determination.

After discussing price economics with the homeowner, I then tell him of the thousands of dwelling units for sale in his marketing area, which is the area a prospective buyer could drive to in 30 minutes. With our freeways, that comprises scores of square miles.

Although his home may be unique in design or location, it is still a dwelling unit. Most of the other homeowners who have their homes for sale have employed professional real estate help.

I point this out to my seller. I impress on him the extreme competitive market he is entering. It is only logical that he should exercise care and sound business judgment in setting the price of his home. I explain that the function of scarcity is working against him. He should know this. He should know its importance, so I tell him!

Fair Median Price

Back to our discussion with the homeowner. If the seller should be coy when I ask him to set the price, and insist that I set the price, I would answer thus.

"Mr. Wilson, considering similar properties, a fair median price for your home would be X number of dollars."

I must have a good idea of its value. I am forcing the seller to commit himself. I would, at this time, wait for the reaction of the seller.

Unfortunately for the real estate lister, unless the price he quoted was nearly identical to the price the seller conjured in his mind, the seller will tell the lister his price is inaccurate and consider the interview terminated. But this is just what I wanted. The home-owner will now tell me just what price he does have in mind.

> Mr. Wilson, the price I mentioned was, as I said, a MEDIAN price. That means it is only a sample price within a range of acceptable prices. A buyer could pay more or he might pay less. No one can say just what a buyer will pay. We don't want to exceed that upper limit nor go below the lower limit. The higher the price, the more sales resistance we shall encounter. The price you mention is well within reason. Let's try it!

Now the professional lister will want to strengthen his image as a knowledgeable calculator of price. I tell this story which meets with great interest.

> You know, Mr. Wilson, setting price on anything is a nebulous task at best. I recall a classic example of price setting I read about some time ago.
> Seems the Coca Cola people wanted to expand their market to South America, so they made a market survey and found that the people there liked their product very much.
> In due course, they set up dispensing machines in the lobbies of the large hotels in the principal cities. Can you guess what happened? They sold hardly a bottle of Coke for months. They couldn't imagine what was wrong. After all, they had a product that had an established quality, price, and acceptance. There should have been no difficulty whatsoever.
> Finally, one of their people came up with the idea of raising the price from five cents to ten cents. From that day on, Coca Cola has been a tremendous success in South America. It seemed that the local people felt that if the product came from the United States, it should cost more. They weren't going to buy a local imitation for a nickel!
> This doesn't mean that you, Mr. Wilson, should raise your price if your home doesn't sell quickly. The Coca Cola people had product scarcity on their side. It just points out how difficult it is to predict what an unknown person will pay for a given product, even a product as apparently easily priced as Coca Cola.
> It behooves you to be very careful, to weigh all factors in your mind before you set a price on your home.

The professional lister should afford the seller a thorough education on pricing of homes similar to his own. The more thorough the education, the fewer problems will the agent have with the seller if the home doesn't sell rapidly.

A Question of Semantics. The question of "overpriced" listings is actually one of semantics. A listing that is truly overpriced is one that does not sell in a reasonable period of time and all other factors, such as location and condition, are normal.

A listing that does not sell is of little benefit to the real estate lister. However, a listing that is suspected of being overpriced, but eventually sells, proves it was not overpriced after all. Rather, the real estate appraiser was "underinformed."

The true price of any listing is precisely what some buyer will pay for it. Hence, it is dangerous to classify a listing as overpriced until it does, or does not, sell after a reasonable time.

As a final thought on pricing, I want you to be aware of another truism:

> Real estate agents are always the last people to realize prices have gone up in an area.

Real estate people often don't keep pace with change. Their appraisal of a home is based on prices a year or two old. Don't you make this fatal mistake. I would rather be a lister than an appraiser! I will make more money, and so will you.

(See THE LISTING MASTER – Gael Himmah Publishing Company – for a condensed, easy to learn pricing dialogue.)

The Facts of
Real Estate Finance

5

<small>DURING THE COURSE</small>
of most conversations with homeowners, the discussion will eventu-

ally turn to matters related to the specifics of real estate finance. The following information will give you a basic working knowledge of finance so you will be able to speak on the subject with confidence.

Mortgage markets are usually classified as primary and secondary markets. The primary market is made up of all lenders who supply funds directly to borrowers, bear the risks associated with long-term financing, and who, as a rule, hold the mortgage until the debt obligation is discharged.

The secondary market is one in which existing mortgages are bought, sold, or borrowed against. Secondary mortgage market lenders or investors buy mortgages as long-term investments in competition with other types of securities, such as government or corporate bonds.

Sources of
Mortgage Funds

Most loans on all types of real properties are made by a group of financial institutions which are referred to as "institutional lenders." This group is comprised of savings and loan associations, life insurance companies, commercial banks doing a savings business, mutual savings banks and mortgage companies.

In addition, there are important non-supervised sources of mortgage funds.

Savings and Loan Companies. The federal government has a very necessary role in real estate finance. The Government wants to insure a continuous flow of credit and provide safeguards to protect the source of savings.

In 1932, the Home Loan Bank Act established the Federal Home Loan Bank. This bank is related to savings and loan associations as the Federal Reserve Bank is related to the commercial banks. Among institutional lenders, savings and loan associations account for the greatest share of the home loan market. They account, nationally, for about one-third of all home loans being made. They act both as a depository for monies saved, and as a source of funds for mortgage loans.

Since the money that is deposited in savings and loan associations is long-term savings investment money, which is expected to earn high interest benefits, the savings and loan associations put almost all of their money into mortgage loans. They usually pay a dividend rate on savings about 2% below their prevailing mortgage loan rate.

There are two kinds of savings and loan associations. Federally chartered savings and loan companies are governed by regulations of the Federal Home Loan Bank Board. They are mutual in nature. This means they are owned by their depositors. The state savings and loan companies are stock companies owned by those persons holding shares of capital stock. A charter for their operation is issued to the stockholders by the state.

Both the federal and state savings and loan companies can make amortized first-mortgage loans for a maximum term of 30 years. The maximum mortgage loan amounts permitted savings and loan associations are 95% of the appraised value of the real property.

Insurance Companies. Insurance companies are another important source of mortgage loan funds. For total mortgage investments, including loans on business and large commercial properties, life insurance companies ranked first among institutional lenders for years. In the competitive loan market, such as in 1961–1963, they are hard-pressed in a race for first place by the eastern savings banks and savings and loan associations.

They differ from the other types of institutional lenders in that their money does not come from deposits. Their money comes from premiums. Hence, they don't have to worry about withdrawals. They are not concerned with liquidity since they can accurately predict their money demands. Thus, insurance companies can make loans other lenders wouldn't consider. They like to make large, long-term loans due to their freedom from savings problems.

They invest on a "prudent man" theory. They can make any investment an individual could make with his own funds if he were a prudent man. They can buy common stocks and raw land. They cannot, however, make loans on unimproved property. Suffice it to say that insurance companies are very flexible in the type of loan they can make. In most states, they can lend up to 75% of the appraised value of the property for a maximum term of 30 years.

Real estate loans placed with life insurance companies are generally for the following purposes:

(1) Purchase money—for occupancy or investment.
(2) Construction loans, or improvement loans.
(3) Refinancing existing indebtedness.
(4) Consolidation of mortgages.
(5) Achieving a lower interest rate or longer term.
(6) Provision for additional funds.

Commercial Banks. Federal statutes regulate national banks and state laws limit the activities of state chartered banks. Limitations may differ between the two types of banks. Mortgage lending policies of individual commercial banks differ widely, depending on the size of bank operations and the community's financial needs.

Fully amortized conventional loans made by all national and state chartered banks are limited to 90% of the appraised value of the security and may extend over a period to a maximum of 30 years. The actual amount a commercial bank will loan, however, varies considerably according to the type of property involved. Commercial banks are a reservoir for commercial lending. Their funds are liquid cash on demand. Hence, they prefer loans that will pay out readily. They usually do not impose pay-off penalties on their loans.

Mutual Savings Banks. Mutual savings banks are one of the oldest forms of banking systems. They have no capital stock, but are mutual in character, and depositors share in the earnings of the bank after allowance for expenses, reserves, and contributions to surplus or guarantee fund. They are operated by a Board of Trustees.

This type of bank functions only in 17 States, most of which are located in the northeastern part of the country. They make very few loans themselves but are very active in the secondary market. They would rather purchase loans that have already been made. Hence, they buy many government-insured loans from loan correspondents. They give loan preference to single family residences.

Mortgage Companies. Mortgage companies throughout the country have occupied a significant role in helping large numbers of individuals and institutions to finance the purchase of real estate. Acting as mortgage loan correspondents for life insurance companies and other financial institutions, these companies do a major share of the home, apartment, store and factory financing of this country.

Other Sources. There are many non-supervised sources of mortgage loan money such as credit unions, title insurance companies in many states, pension and welfare funds, university and college endowment funds, perpetual care funds of cemeteries, individuals and estates, and trade unions.

Federal Participation in Real Estate Finance

FHA Program. In the real estate business, we need federal mortgage guarantees in order to ease the flow of money across state lines, to make available high percentage loans, and to cover the risks of high percentage loans that can be insured only by the body that controls the nation's credit, namely, the federal government.

The National Housing Act of 1934 gave birth to the FHA, which deals only with lenders approved by the FHA. These approved lenders are composed of all member banks of the Federal Reserve System, all member banks of the Federal Deposit Insurance Corporation, all mutual savings banks, all savings and loan associations, all life insurance companies, and any corporation with $100,000 of paid in capital that is doing business as a bona fide lending company.

There are several different types of FHA insured loans. We shall discuss only that type related to the financing of real property purchases.

There are definite loan limitations under the FHA program that are varied from time to time by Congress. The maximum amount of money that can currently be loaned and insured for a single family dwelling is $45,000; for a duplex, $48,750; for a triplex, $48,750; and for a fourplex, $56,000.

The FHA has established a ratio of loan amount to appraised value. For a single family dwelling, the FHA will insure a loan of 97%

of the first $25,000 of appraised value; 90% of the next $10,000 of appraised value; and 80% of the balance of appraised value to a maximum loan amount of $45,000.

If the residence to be financed was not built under FHA supervision and it is less than one year old, the FHA loan limits are 90% of what the loan would have been if it was a regular FHA loan—as shown in the preceding paragraph.

If the property to be purchased is not going to be occupied by the owner, the FHA will only insure a loan of 85% of what the loan would have been if the property was owner-occupied.

The current rate of interest charged a borrower on a FHA loan is 8¾%. In addition, the borrower must pay ½% mutual mortgage insurance. This insurance names the lender as beneficiary, and protects the lender against dollar loss should the property be foreclosed upon at some later date.

Some of the outstanding features of the FHA loan program are:

(a) The specified ratio of loan amount to appraised value must be maintained at all times.

(b) Maturity of the loan can be as long as 40 years.

(c) The note must include a prepayment privilege without penalty.

(d) The note must contain a non-acceleration clause and waiver of prepayment penalty in the event the title is transferred.

(e) No secondary financing is permitted.

For a buyer to qualify to purchase under the FHA program, the purchaser must have a gross monthly income approximately five times greater than the monthly mortgage payments which include principal, interest, taxes and insurance.

The foreclosure procedure under FHA financing is interesting. The lender must notify the FHA that the loan is in default. The lender must start the foreclosure proceedings himself. If the default is not cured within one year and foreclosure is not started within that time, the mortgage insurance is no longer in effect, so it behooves the lender to start the foreclosure proceedings promptly.

If, at the foreclosure sale, the lender is awarded the property, he has 30 days to decide whether he will turn the property over to the FHA, sell it on the open market, or keep it.

If the lender chooses to take advantage of his FHA insurance, he must be able to deliver to the FHA good title, no waste or damage, and occupancy. Upon delivery of the property to the FHA, the FHA delivers debenture bonds to the lender. These debenture bonds cover the principal unpaid balance of the loan, any taxes paid by the lender, and interest from the start of foreclosure at the debenture rate.

The lender can, if he chooses, file a claim for interest and expenses for the period from default to the start of foreclosure in a certificate of claim. The FHA then readies the home and lists it with a real estate broker for sale. If the FHA can sell the house for a profit, any residue is applied to the certificate of claim.

VA Program. The Veteran's Administration home loan program is part of the Serviceman's Readjustment Act of 1944. This program guarantees loans for businesses, farms and homes.

In 1974, the VA raised their guarantee limits to 60% of the loan requested, not to exceed a maximum guarantee of $17,500.

For example, say we have a VA appraisal on a home of $30,000. A lender who, by statute, could only lend two-thirds of their appraisal, a national bank let's say, would normally be able to lend $20,000 on this property. But since this property is to be purchased under the terms of a GI (VA) loan and the lender is guaranteed against loss for a maximum of $17,500, he can add the amount of the guarantee to what he could normally lend. Hence, the bank adds $17,500 to the $20,000 sum, and could therefore lend $37,500 on the property. Since only $30,000 is required for purchase, we see that the veteran buyer could buy the home with no down payment.

The sales price of a home to be purchased under the GI program must not exceed the reasonable value (current market value) as established by a VA appraiser. This VA appraisal figure is issued on a form called a Certificate of Reasonable Value. The CRV figure must be high enough to cover the sales price, the cost of any termite work required, and the cost of any bonds or assessments against the property.

Some of the outstanding features of the VA loan program are:

(a) No down payment is required.

(b) Maturity of the loan is 30 years.

(c) The note must include a prepayment privilege without penalty.

(d) The note must include a non-acceleration clause in the event of the transfer of title.

(e) Eligible properties are one to four family dwellings only.

(f) No secondary financing is permitted.

A lender goes through three basic steps in processing a VA loan. First, he must get a CRV on the property to be purchased. This qualifies the property. Next, he must get a certificate of eligibility from the VA showing the purchaser to be eligible to purchase under the VA program. This qualifies the buyer. Finally, the lender requests a certificate of commitment. This qualifies the deal. This commitment certificate comes from the VA which has to approve the credit of the buyer and the value of the property.

The buyer must have a net monthly income that is at least four and a half times greater than the proposed monthly mortgage payment including principal, interest, taxes and insurance.

The foreclosure procedure under the VA program differs from that of the FHA.

The VA does not pay off the lender in debenture bonds in the event of loss, as does the FHA. The VA pays off in cash.

When a loan is in default, the lender must wait 60 days and then notify the VA. The VA sends someone out to contact the borrower. If the lender and the VA decide nothing can be done to make the loan current, the VA will make the decision to start foreclosure proceedings. Only the VA can make this decision.

The VA gives the lender an "upset price," which is the price the lender bids at the foreclosure sale. The upset price includes expenses and accrued outstanding interest and principal on the loan. The VA pays the lender the upset price.

Learn all you can about conventional and government-insured financing. Learn every detail. Make it your business to do so promptly; it is vital to listing success.

Listing Forms
and Definitions

6

A LISTING IS A UNI-
lateral contract. This, by definition, means one-sided. It is under-

taken by one of two or more parties to the contract. The seller agrees to pay the listing agent a sum of money, the commission, only if the agent performs according to the terms of the contract.

An agent holding a listing—exclusive, non-exclusive, open, or net—is always bound by the law of agency and has certain obligations to his principal that do not exist between two principals.

The agent owes his client a definite loyalty, and he is prohibited by law from personal profiting by virtue of his agency, except by the agreed compensation for his services. The fiduciary character of the agent's position is the most important phase of the relationship. An agent cannot receive any secret profits adverse to his principal. An agent must also inform his principal of every fact material to the advantage of the principal.

Basic Listing
Definitions

There are five types of listings in normal real estate usage: exclusive right to sell, exclusive agency, net, open, and multiple listings.

Exclusive Right to Sell Listing. An exclusive right to sell listing specifies that a commission is due the broker named in the listing if, during the term of the listing, the property is sold by the named broker, by any other broker, by the property owner, or if the property is withdrawn from sale, transferred, conveyed, or leased without approval of the agent. A definite termination date is an essential. This type of listing affords the agent the greatest protection and should be the goal of every listing specialist.

Exclusive Agency Listing. An exclusive agency listing is a contract wherein the property owner consents to a specifically named real estate broker being his exclusive agent and agrees to pay the named agent a specified commission if he produces a buyer "ready, willing, and able" to buy the property according to the terms and conditions specified by the property owner.

However, the property owner reserves the right to sell his property himself, to purchasers he might obtain through his own efforts, and should he do so, he is not obligated to pay the agent a commission. An exclusive agency listing should have a specified termination date.

The following clause should be present in an exclusive agency listing:

This is an exclusive agency listing.
Seller is not obligated to the commission statement for buyers he should secure through his own efforts.

Exclusive agency listings are so important to the successful lister that I have devoted an entire chapter to their use. (*See* Chapter 16.)

Net Listing. A net listing is an authorization to sell given an agent by a principal wherein the amount of compensation is not precisely determined, but a clause in the contract usually permits the agent to retain as compensation all the money received in excess of a specified sum set by the seller.

Although perfectly legal, a net listing may give rise to charges of fraud, misrepresentation, and other abuses because of its loosely defined commission clause. A seller, happy with a net listing at the time he signs it, often becomes bitter when the agent sells the property for a great deal more than the net figure and the agent realizes an unusually generous compensation. Because of this, I do not recommend the use of net listings. An excellent alternative, with benefits to both agent and principal, is the 90% listing arrangement discussed in Chapter 13.

Open Listing. An open listing is a written memorandum signed by the seller of the property which authorizes the real estate licensee to act as his agent for the sale of his property.

A definite time limit is not an essential although many open listings provide for a definite term. There should be an adequate description of the property, and the terms and conditions of sale should be defined.

Open listings are the most elementary form of written authorization. They may be given concurrently to more than one agent, and usually the seller is not required to notify the other agents in case of a sale by one of them in order to prevent liability of paying more than one commission. The sale of the property under such an agreement is considered to cancel all outstanding listings.

Where several open listings have been given by the property owner, the agent who produces an acceptable sales contract receives all the commission. If the property owner sells the property himself, he is not obligated to pay any commission and all open listings are automatically canceled.

Multiple Listing. In many areas of the country, cooperating real estate offices have joined together, in most cases through local real estate boards, to form a multiple listing service whereby the member offices share their listings with each other.

When a member firm gets a new listing, he submits it to the multiple listing service which, in turn, prints informational copies of the listing and distributes it to the other member firms. If the listing is sold by a cooperating member office, the cooperating office receives a percentage of the gross commission and the listing office gets the balance of the commission.

It is easily seen how a salesman who becomes a professional lister, and who submits a continual flow of new listings to the multiple listing service, will have an unending source of income. He has many salesmen working on his listings, trying their best to make a sale.

I always recommend multiple listing to homeowners. They enjoy the greater sales exposure of many brokers working to produce a sale on their property. I like the odds of having all the members of my local multiple listing service working to sell my listings.

Listing
Forms

Exclusive Right to Sell Listing. Figure 2 is an example of a properly executed exclusive right to sell listing agreement. These forms are usually supplied through local real estate boards or title insurance companies.

The agent should always leave a copy of the completed listing form with the sellers. The location in which the listing contract was signed is entered at the top of the form, followed by the name of the agent. Bonanza Realty, Inc. is a corporation licensed to do business as a real estate broker in California. Hence, Bonanza Realty, Inc., is the agent.

The term of the listing shown in the illustration is nearly seven months. I believe in taking listings for a term long enough to include the estimated time required to procure a buyer, process the loan, and close the escrow. In the case of government-insured financing, this could be longer than seven months.

I often take listings for a year or more. I will not allow myself to develop the habit of taking listings for only 90 days. I do a good job for my clients. I expect protection in return for my professional services. When explained to sellers on these terms, they don't object.

In filling out the form, make certain the agreed upon sales price is both written out and shown in arabic numerals, as if you were making out a check.

Since Lafayette is unincorporated, it cannot be accurately termed a city. Hence, "area of Lafayette" is inserted in the appropriate space rather than "city of Lafayette."

A complete legal description of the property to be sold is usually not necessary. The description should be so compete as to leave no room for contention later on. Any personal property included with the real property should be described in the listing contract. Any exceptions or unusual conditions of the property should be included.

On most properties, I believe in agreeing to secure an "all cash" offer for the seller. If the seller will consider carrying secondary financing himself, I would enter this information on the listing form, being careful to include the rate, term, monthly payment, and credit requirement specified by the seller.

"All cash" is not as brutal a requirement as it sounds. "All cash" to the seller is really a combination of a nominal cash down payment and a mortgage loan to the buyer. Psychologically, the ring of "all cash" is a tonic to the seller. I don't believe in wasting time and losing sales advantage by debating possible terms with a seller.

We can't be specific about terms when we take a listing since we don't know what method of financing a prospective buyer will

AUTHORIZATION TO SELL

............Lafayette............, California, ...June 8, 19......

In consideration of the services of............BONANZA REALTY, INC............ hereinafter called the agent, I hereby list with said agent, exclusively and irrevocably, for a period of time beginning ......June 8......, 19...... and ending......December 31......, 19......, and grant said agent the exclusive and irrevocable right to sell within said time for..Twenty Five Thousand and no/100----- ($.25,000,00.- - - -..............) Dollars, and to accept a deposit thereon, the following described property in the Area of Lafayette............County of..Contra Costa............State of California, to-wit:

Lot and improvements commonly known as 875 Oak Street, said sales

price to include the wall to wall carpets in the living room and the

drapes in the living room and family room.

The purchase price shall be payable as follows: All cash to sellers.

Sellers agree to pay a maximum of 2 points for FHA or GI financing.

I hereby agree to pay the agent as commission......SIX..(6)..............per cent of the selling price herein named, whether said property is sold by said agent, or by me, or by another agent, or through some other source, or if said property is transferred, conveyed, leased or withdrawn from sale during the time set forth herein.

If within ten days after the termination of this listing, said agent notifies me in writing personally, or by mail, that during its life, he negotiated with persons named by him, and sale is made within one hundred eighty(180) days after the termination of this contract to any person so named, I agree to pay the agent the commission provided for herein.

If a deposit is forfeited, one-half thereof shall go to said agent as commission and one-half to me, provided, however the agent's share shall not exceed the amount of the above named commission.

Evidence of title to be in the form of a Policy of Title Insurance issued by the LAFAYETTE TITLE COMPANY and paid for by the buyer.

Thirty days allowed for examination of title, following receipt of the deposit. Taxes (July 1 basis), interest, insurance, loan trust funds (if indebtedness is being assumed) and rents to be prorated. Insurance may be cancelled. When sold as herein provided, I will convey said property to the buyer by a grant deed, and when notified of sale I will immediately upon request deposit with said Title Company for delivery, said deed and any other documents and instructions necessary to complete the transaction. If objection to title is reported, I agree to take immediate steps to clear title and buyer shall within five days after title is reported cleared by the Title Company, deposit the full purchase price in escrow.

Notice of sale hereunder may be given to me by telephone, orally, or by mail to the address given below, or by personal service.

Time is of the essence hereof. In the event of the failure of a buyer to perform any of the terms hereof, all rights of such buyer shall immediately cease and terminate.

We hereby acknowledge receipt of a copy of this contract.

Address......875..Oak..Street..

......Lafayette,..California..

Telephone..283-2206..

In consideration of the above listing, the undersigned agent agrees to use diligence in procuring a buyer.

John R. Thatcher

Marie S. Thatcher
Seller.

BONANZA REALTY, INC.

By _Carl C. Finney_
Real Estate Agent.

Figure 2

offer. In addition, the listing agent's primary responsibility is to the seller. By advising him to accept only "all cash," we, as agents, are acting in his best interests.

I have written a sentence on the listing form (Figure 2) committing the seller to pay a specified number of points for government-insured financing.

Of course, I don't use the sentence if the property is such that it will not, or cannot, be financed under the FHA or GI programs. But if the possibility of government-insured financing exists, I inform my sellers of this and tell them the "story of points" detailed in Chapter 3. The sellers should know what to expect in equating a given number of points to dollars out of their pocket. They should not be surprised with this information when the agent presents them with an offer to purchase or, worse yet, when the escrow is about to close and they are asked to sign their sellers' instructions.

The commission agreed upon should be written out and illustrated by arabic numerals. Unclear penmanship has resulted in many an awkward situation.

Of great importance is the second paragraph of the printed terms. This is a clause which protects the agent. It insures him that he will be paid a commission if someone he has shown the property to during the term of the listing buys it after the listing has expired, hoping to prevent the agent from being paid a commission and thereby buying the property for a reduced price. To gain the protection of this clause, the agent must notify the seller in writing personally, or by mail, within ten days after the termination of the listing, that he, the agent, negotiated with persons named by him. If a sale is made within 180 days after the termination of the contract illustrated, to any person so named, the seller agrees to pay the agent the specified commission.

In most listing contracts this protection period is 60 or 90 days. I have seen buyers who were willing to wait 90 days for their "dream house" if they could buy it for 6% less than the price quoted when the agent showed it to them. I have seen sellers who were willing to wait 90 days, especially if their property was meeting sales resistance. They felt another buyer might not come along so they agreed with the agent's customer to wait 90 days from the expiration date of the listing contract, "legally" do the agent out of his "morally earned" commission, and consummate the sale at a reduced price.

This is the precise reason for the 180-day figure. I have never found a buyer who would wait six months. It is unfortunate that conditions are such that this is required for self protection, but such is the case.

A seller who does not intend to cheat an agent out of an earned commission, and this includes most sellers who are more than happy to pay for a job well done, does not object to this 180-day clause. He recognizes its function and knows it will not affect him.

All parties whose names appear on the property deed of ownership must sign the listing form. In many states, one owner can commit himself to paying the agent a commission if a buyer is obtained who is ready, willing, and able to purchase on the exact terms of the listing, but since all owners had not signed the listing, the owners cannot be forced to deliver title.

You can see what problems could result. The prudent lister will be certain he has the signatures of everyone having an ownership interest in the property.

Finally, the listing agent signs the form, agreeing to use "diligence" in procuring a buyer. If the agent did not thereafter, for the term of the listing, make a continuous effort to procure a buyer for the property, he would be guilty of breaching the contract.

The manner in which the listing form (Figure 2) is laid out is excellent in that it affords the listing agent ample space to write. This is much appreciated by listing agents everywhere.

Exclusive Agency Listing. Figure 3 is an example of an exclusive agency listing. We use the standard exclusive right to sell form and amend it with the exclusive agency clause.

In the first sentence at the top of the listing form, the seller has agreed that the listing is "exclusive" and "irrevocable." The handwritten exclusive agency clause overrides this. A contradictory, handwritten (or typed) amendment to a contract, in most instances, supersedes the printed portion.

Net Listing. Figure 4 is an example of a net listing. Again, the ex-

AUTHORIZATION TO SELL

......Walnut Creek...... California, ... August 1, 19......

In consideration of the services of........ BONANZA REALTY, INC. ....

hereinafter called the agent, I hereby list with said agent, exclusively and irrevocably, for a period of time beginning ......August 1...... 19...... and ending......March 15...... 19......, and grant said agent the exclusive and irrevocable right to sell within said time for......Thirty Seven Thousand and no/100..........

($.37,000.00......) Dollars, and to accept a deposit thereon, the following described property in the City of Walnut Creek......County of..Contra Costa..............State of California, to-wit:

Lot and improvements commonly known as 115 Darien Road.

The purchase price shall be payable as follows: All cash to sellers.

This is an EXCLUSIVE AGENCY listing. Sellers are not obligated to the commission statement for buyers they should secure through their own efforts.

I hereby agree to pay the agent as commission ....SIX. (6).............per cent of the selling price herein named, whether said property is sold by said agent, or by me, or by another agent, or through some other source, or if said property is transferred, conveyed, leased or withdrawn from sale during the time set forth herein.

If within ten days after the termination of this listing, said agent notifies me in writing personally, or by mail, that during its life, he negotiated with persons named by him, and sale is made within one hundred eighty(180) days after the termination of this contract to any person so named, I agree to pay the agent the commission provided for herein.

If a deposit is forfeited, one-half thereof shall go to said agent as commission and one-half to me, provided, however the agent's share shall not exceed the amount of the above named commission.

Evidence of title to be in the form of a Policy of Title Insurance issued by the LAFAYETTE TITLE COMPANY and paid for by the buyer.

Thirty days allowed for examination of title, following receipt of the deposit. Taxes (July 1 basis), interest, insurance, loan trust funds (if indebtedness is being assumed) and rents to be prorated. Insurance may be cancelled. When sold as herein provided, I will convey said property to the buyer by a grant deed, and when notified of sale I will immediately upon request deposit with said Title Company for delivery, said deed and any other documents and instructions necessary to complete the transaction. If objection to title is reported, I agree to take immediate steps to clear title and buyer shall within five days after title is reported cleared by the Title Company, deposit the full purchase price in escrow.

Notice of sale hereunder may be given to me by telephone, orally, or by mail to the address given below, or by personal service.

Time is of the essence hereof. In the event of the failure of a buyer to perform any of the terms hereof, all rights of such buyer shall immediately cease and terminate.

We hereby acknowledge receipt of a copy of this contract.

Address ....115 Darien Road..

......Walnut Creek, California..

Telephone ....934-1011..

Howard K. Vessing

Jayce A. Vessing

Seller.

In consideration of the above listing, the undersigned agent agrees to use diligence in procuring a buyer.

BONANZA REALTY, INC.

By _Jack C. Hummel_

Real Estate Agent.

Figure 3

AUTHORIZATION TO SELL

................San Francisco.............., California, ...May 22, 19.......

In consideration of the services of....BONANZA REALTY, INC.,............................
hereinafter called the agent, I hereby list with said agent, exclusively and irrevocably, for a period of time beginning
........May 22........, 19......... and ending.........August 31........, 19......, and grant said agent the
exclusive and irrevocable right to sell within said time for........SEE BELOW...
($..SEE BELOW...........) Dollars, and to accept a deposit thereon, the following described property in the
City of San Francisco........County of....San Francisco.................................State of California, to-wit:

Lot and improvements commonly known as 2115 Octavia Street.

The purchase price shall be payable as follows: This is a NET listing. Seller to receive

Forty Seven Thousand and no/100 ($47,000.00) dollars from the sale of

the above described property. Seller agrees to pay seller's normal

closing costs. Agent to retain as commission balance of sales price

above $47,000.

I hereby agree to pay the agent as commission......SEE ABOVE.....~~ten per cent of the selling price of said property,~~ **GCH AAT** whether said property is sold by said agent, or by me, or by another agent, or through some other source, or if said property is transferred, conveyed, leased or withdrawn from sale during the time set forth herein.

If within ten days after the termination of this listing, said agent notifies me in writing personally, or by mail, that during its life, he negotiated with persons named by him, and sale is made within one hundred eighty(180) days after the termination of this contract to any person so named, I agree to pay the agent the commission provided for herein.

If a deposit is forfeited, one-half thereof shall go to said agent as commission and one-half to me, provided, however the agent's share shall not exceed the amount of the above named commission.

Evidence of title to be in the form of a Policy of Title Insurance issued by.........any.........TITLE COMPANY and paid for by the buyer.

Thirty days allowed for examination of title, following receipt of the deposit. Taxes (July 1 basis), interest, insurance, loan trust funds (if indebtedness is being assumed) and rents to be prorated. Insurance may be cancelled. When sold as herein provided, I will convey said property to the buyer by a grant deed, and when notified of sale I will immediately, upon request deposit with said Title Company for delivery, said deed and any other documents and instructions necessary to complete the transaction. If objection to title is reported, I agree to take immediate steps to clear title and buyer shall within five days after title is reported cleared by the Title Company, deposit the full purchase price in escrow.

Notice of sale hereunder may be given to me by telephone, orally, or by mail to the address given below, or by personal service.

Time is of the essence hereof. In the event of the failure of a buyer to perform any of the terms hereof, all rights of such buyer shall immediately cease and terminate.

We hereby acknowledge receipt of a copy of this contract.

Address...2115 Octavia Street.................................

....San Francisco, California...................................

Telephone...TU 7-6562..................................

    ....*Albert A. Turner*.........................
                        (His separate property)

    .... **Seller.**

In consideration of the above listing, the undersigned agent agrees to use diligence in procuring a buyer.

                        BONANZA REALTY, INC.

    By...........*Joel Coffman*...........
                        Real Estate Agent.

Figure 4

clusive right to sell listing form is used and is amended as illustrated.

Note that both the agent and the seller have initialed the portion of the contract that has been lined out; a part of the line defining the commission obligation of the seller.

Note also, at the bottom of the form, there is only one signature by the seller and a statement entered under it advising that the described real estate is his separate property. A statement of explanation should always be included if only one seller's signature is shown.

Open Listing. As previously mentioned, an open listing is merely a written memorandum. Figure 5 is an example.

In this example a termination date is shown, but it is not necessary to make the listing binding.

Multiple Listing. Figure 6 is an example of a multiple listing form properly filled out. A detailed discussion of filling in the informational section can be found in Chapter 17.

Multiple listing forms vary among real estate boards. It is important to note that the information-description section at the top half of the form is not a part of the contract. It is only a convenient place to set down a description of the property. Under normal circumstances, the real estate agent cannot be held liable for errors in this section.

The lower portion of the form is the contractual section. The terms are similar to those in the exclusive right to sell form. In fact, a multiple listing is an exclusive right to sell listing that is submitted to the multiple listing service for distribution to the cooperating broker members. Regardless of which broker actually procures a buyer, the seller is committed to pay a commission only to the broker whose name is on the multiple listing contract.

This listing broker, by subscribing to the by-laws of the multiple listing service, has previously agreed to the method of dividing the commission between himself and the selling broker.

Combination Listing Form. Many real estate offices have printed their own listing forms. At Bonanza Realty, Inc. we have done so. We have devised an exclusive right to sell listing form that doubles as a multiple listing and can be easily amended to become an exclusive agency listing by adding the exclusive agency clause.

In addition, as you can see in Figure 7, by using our own listing forms we have an opportunity to do some advertising about the many services Bonanza Realty, Inc. has to offer.

Our office listing forms are printed on "chemical" paper so that carbon paper is not required between copies. You can see how closely our listing form resembles the multiple listing service form.

Our multiple listing service does not require that listings submitted to it be filled out on multiple listing service forms although the forms are available. As long as all the required information is submitted and the listing contract is properly executed, our multiple listing service will accept it for distribution.

NON EXCLUSIVE OPEN LISTING

Date January 5, 19

Price $21,500.00   Terms All cash to seller

Location 315 Gran Via, Alamo, California

General Description:

Lot and improvements commonly known as 315 Gran Via, Alamo,

California, sales price to include all carpets and drapes

in house and all swimming pool equipment.

_____

_____

_____

_____

_____

_____

_____

First Loan $ 8,216.88 Int. 6¼ % Payable $ 104.00 A mo.(and)(incl.) Int.

Second Loan $ none Int. ____ % Payable $ ____ A mo.(and)(incl.) Int.

TO: BONANZA REALTY, INC. Licensed Real Estate Broker

You are given the non exclusive right to sell the property described above upon the price and terms as written and you are hereby authorized to accept a deposit thereon. Should you secure a purchaser ready, willing and able to purchase said property upon said price and terms, or other price and terms which I accept or should I sell or exchange said property to anyone whose attention was brought to said property as a result of your efforts.

I will pay you a commission of SIX (6) percent of the selling price and I hereby acknowledge receipt of a copy of this listing.

This Listing Terminates February 29 19 ____

LISTING ACCEPTED: Signed *Randall W. Watson*

Date January 5 ,19 ____ Signed *Velma R. Watson*
(owner)

BONANZA REALTY, INC. Address 315 Gran Via, Alamo
Licensed Real Estate Broker

By _____ Telephone VE 7-9927

Figure 5

CONTRA COSTA MULTIPLE LISTING SERVICE

EXCLUSIVE LISTING DATED ____February 2____ 19___

Subject to conditions hereinafter set forth

NO LISTING ACCEPTED FOR LESS THAN 90 DAYS

The Mart Copy of This Listing Must Be Turned in to the Multiple Office by the Listing Office Within 48 Hours After Being Signed by the Owner

Date __2/2/__ HOME Listing # ____

Address __2516 March Road, Concord__ Price $ __25,500__

Area or Subd. __off Galindo St. near Park Road__ Style __Alpine__

Occupied by __Owner__ Phone ____ Ext. __Redwood__

Owner __Mason, Dr. J.B.__ Phone __685-1758__

Address __Same__ Roof __Shingle__

Listing Office __Bonanza Realty (Himmah)__ Phone __284-1122__ Gar. __double__

How Shown __Phone for appointment - LOKBOX__ Floors __hardwood__

Reason for Selling __moving to New York__ Fireplace __4__

Occupancy Date __By agreement__ Zoning ____ Heat __Central__

Terms of Sale __Cash to best loan__ Dining __area__

Present Loan $ __Clear__ for ____ yrs. @ ____ % Pmt. $ ____ Brkfst. __kitchen__

Pmt. inc. $ ____ Ins.; $ ____ Taxes; $ ____ Assmt. Laundry __Garage__

Loan Commitment $ __20,400__ for __25__ yrs. @ __6__ % Pmt. $ __131.45__ Shower __2 stalls__

Sewer There? __yes__ Connected __yes__ Bal. Assmt. $ __none__ Elect. Kit. X, R&O X

Lot Size __Apx 1/3 A F 100 s152 R106 s141 Contour level__ Dsp. X, D.W. X Ref.,

Remarks __SPEECHLESS!! You can't believe the view__ Taxes __506__

__It's magnificent. An authentic sportsman's__ Vet. Ex. __no__

__lodge. Extreme seclusion. A forest hide-__

__away. Giant oaks & pines. Flagstone fireplaces.__

ADDRESS	CITY	STORY	ROOMS	BEDRMS	BATH	AGE	PRICE
2516 March Road	C	1	7	3	3	11	$ 25,500

In consideration of services to be performed by __BONANZA REALTY, INC.__, hereinafter called Broker, I hereby employ Broker as my sole and exclusive agent to sell for me that certain real property situated in the City of __Concord__, County of Contra Costa, California, as above described. I hereby grant said Broker the exclusive and irrevocable right to sell the same, and to accept a deposit thereon, for the price of $ __25,500__ on the following terms: $ __all__ ____ cash; balance payable $ ____

This authority shall continue irrevocably from date until terminated on ____November 30____, 19____

I agree to pay Broker __5__ per cent of the selling price in the event that during the period of this contract:

Broker secures a purchaser ready, able and willing to purchase said property on the above terms, or at any other price or terms acceptable to me, or said property is sold or exchanged or leased by said broker or any other person, including myself. I agree to pay Broker said per cent of the listing price if I withdraw said property from sale or exchange, or otherwise prevent performance hereunder by Broker

I agree to pay Broker said percent of the selling price if said property be sold or exchanged within three months after the termination of this contract to any person with whom Broker has negotiated or to whose attention he has called said property and whose name has, during the life hereof or within ten days after its termination, been submitted to me in writing personally or by mail to me at my address given below, in which case Broker shall be conclusively deemed the procuring cause of such sale or lease or exchange to such person.

It is understood Broker is a broker member of Contra Costa Real Estate Board. Members of said Board may act in association with Broker in procuring or attempting to procure a purchaser. This shall not be construed as making the Board my agent for any purpose, or as making any members sub-agents of the Board or of Broker. In the event a sale or exchange shall be made or a purchaser procured by a member of the Board other than Broker, all of the terms of this agreement shall apply to the transaction, subject to the rights of Broker. Payment for commission or compensation hereunder shall be made by me only to Broker.

Evidence of merchantable title shall be in form of policy of title insurance by a responsible title company, same to be paid for by purchaser.

Interest, insurance, taxes, expenses and rent shall be pro-rated through escrow as of date of recording of deed, unless otherwise herein designated.

In case deposit is forfeited, one-half of same shall be retained by or paid to Broker as his compensation, and one-half to me, provided Broker's portion of any forfeiture shall not exceed the amount of the above named commission. (IN TRIPLICATE)

RECEIPT OF A COPY OF THIS LISTING IS HEREBY ACKNOWLEDGED.

(Signed) _Laura B. Moss, M.D._, Owner

Lois R. Moss, Owner

2516 March Road, Concord Address

IN CONSIDERATION OF THE ABOVE EMPLOYMENT, BROKER AGREES TO USE DILIGENCE IN PROCURING A PURCHASER

Broker _BONANZA REALTY, INC._ Address _Lafayette, California_

By _[signature]_

(Dated _February 2_, 19____)

Figure 6

BONANZA REALTY, INC.

EXCLUSIVE LISTING AGREEMENT

BONANZA REALTY

SERVICES INCLUDE:

- Multiple Listing — Contra Costa Board of Realtors
- Assured Sales Plan Trades
- Special Property Brochures
- Nation-wide Exchanges
- Professional Counselling
- Merchandising Services
- Mortgage Financing Assistance
- A Complete Selection of New and Used Residential Properties
- Insurance Counselling
- Investment Properties
- Commercial Developments

TERMS AND CONDITIONS

EXCLUSIVE LISTING DATED.................... Subject to conditions hereinafter set forth ....19......

Date	Price $
Address	Sq. Ft. (House)
Area or Subd.	Style
Occupied by _____ Phone	Ext.
Owner _____ Phone	
Address	Roof
Listing Salesman	Gar.
How Shown	Floors
Reason for Selling	Fireplace
Occupancy Date	Heat
Terms of Sale _____ Zoning	Dining
Present Loan $ _____ for _____ yrs. at _____ % Pmt. $	Brkfst.
Pmt. inc. $ _____ Ins.; $ _____ Taxes; $ _____ Assmt.	Laundry
Loan Commitment $ _____ for _____ yrs. at _____ % Pmt. $	Shower.
Sewer There? _____ Connected _____ Bal. Assmt. $	Elec. Kit. __ R&O
Lot Size _____ F __ S __ R __ S __ Contour	Dsp. __ D.W. __ Ref.
Remarks	Fmly Rm
	Taxes
	Vet. Ex.

ADDRESS	CITY	STORY	ROOMS	BEDRMS	BATH	AGE	PRICE

HOME Listing #

In consideration of services to be performed by Bonanza Realty, Inc., hereinafter called Broker, I hereby employ Broker as my sole and exclusive agent to sell for me that certain real property situated in the city of _____, County of Contra Costa, California, as above described. I hereby grant said Broker the exclusive and irrevocable right to sell the same, and to accept a deposit thereon, for the price of $_____on the following terms:

$_____ cash; balance payable $_____

....

This authority shall continue irrevocably from date until terminated on _____, 19_____.

I agree to pay Bonanza Realty, Inc., as commission_____per cent of the selling price should, during the time set forth herein, said property be sold by said broker or by me or by another broker or through some other source or whether said property be withdrawn from sale, transferred, conveyed, or leased without approval of Bonanza Realty, Inc.

I agree to pay Bonanza Realty, Inc., said per cent of the selling price if said property be sold or exchanged within 180 days after the termination of this contract to any person, with whom Broker has negotiated prior to whose attention he has called said property and whose name has, during the life hereof or within ten days after its termination, been submitted to me in writing personally or by mail to me at my address given below, in which case Broker shall be conclusively deemed the procuring cause of such sale or lease or exchange to such person.

In the event of a sale or exchange of my property I agree to execute and deliver a deed, or such other instrument as may be required. I shall provide evidence of merchantable title in form of policy of title insurance by a responsible title company, same to be paid for by purchaser.

Interest, insurance, taxes, expenses and rent shall be prorated through escrow as of date of recording of deed, unless otherwise herein designated.

In case deposit is forfeited, one-half of same shall be retained by or paid to Broker as his compensation, and one-half to me, provided Broker's portion of any forfeiture shall not exceed the amount of the above named commission.

In consideration of the above employment, Bonanza Realty, Inc., agrees to use due diligence in procuring a purchaser and to include any of the specialized services listed at the agent's discretion that will assist in satisfactorily consummating a transaction for and on behalf of the seller. Owner acknowledges receipt of a copy of this agreement.

Dated at _____ [Signed] _____, Owner

this _____ day of _____, 19_____ [Signed] _____, Owner

By _____ _____, Address
       (salesman)

Ask about Assured Sales Plan. It's the easy way to a new home. ASP gives you:
1. **PEACE OF MIND:** You always know in advance the most and least you will receive for your home.
2. **MONEY:** You save many of the costs of selling and buying by combining them under one transaction.
3. **TIME:** ASP relieves the uncertainties of moving dates, school registration and employment deadlines.
4. **CONVENIENCE:** The management of the complex problems of real estate transfers are handled by experts.
5. **SECURITY:** With ASP you know that your valuable real estate is guarded from bargain hunting speculators.

Figure 7

Sources of
Profitable Listings

7

sources of listings. The most fruitful are herein described.

Expired Multiple Listings. In many instances multiple listings expire without having sold. After the termination date on the listing contract has passed, the listing becomes a property "up for grabs," so to speak.

Many multiple listing services regularly publish lists of expired listings for the information of all the member offices. This is a wonderful source of listings since the sellers are conditioned to dealing with agents. I will discuss methods of developing expired multiple listing leads by use of the telephone in Chapter 8.

For Sale by Owner Signs. A short drive through almost any city's residential neighborhood will reveal a number of homes displaying "For Sale" signs.

This is an excellent source of listings. The homeowner is advising the entire populace that he wants to sell his home. He is so anxious to sell that he has taken the trouble to construct a sign and hammer it into his front lawn. Down deep in his heart he knows his chances of success are remote, but he's going to try for awhile anyway.

For Sale by Owner Ads in Newspapers. When an owner begins spending his hard earned money to pay for newspaper advertisements, the professional lister begins to count his commission money. Newspaper advertising is expensive. A homeowner who spends his own money advertising is really anxious to sell. He can hardly wait!

In many cases, the advertisement will give the address of the home. If it does not, the address is quite easy to obtain. The seller has purposefully omitted the address in order to screen out real estate agents when they call for information.

When you dial the number, introduce yourself as a real estate salesman but act as if you were just another shopper. Begin asking questions about the house. Then say you'd like to stop by later in the day. The address will be made very clear. The seller will see to that. After all, you sounded like a buyer.

Should the seller say he doesn't want to talk to a real estate agent, you can reply that you often act as a principal, purchasing properties directly from owners for resale in the future. When you arrive at the house you will find a warm welcome waiting you. The seller feels you still might buy the house.

After an inspection of the home, if you decide you wouldn't want to own this property, you can explain that the house is not exactly what you had in mind and if you made them an offer to purchase, the sellers would actually realize less cash than if you sold it for them through normal real estate channels. This is your entry into your listing presentation, which will be discussed in detail in following chapters.

Door to Door Canvass. Many real estate brokers recommend door to door "cold" canvassing of neighborhoods as the most satisfactory method of obtaining listings. Certainly the doorbell technique has merit. It teaches a salesman self-confidence, and it produces listings, but not in proportion to the effort expended.

I believe door to door canvassing for listings, in the main, wastes time and is non-professional, depressing, and discouraging. There are some salesmen who enjoy cold canvass solicitation. If they are successful in getting listings this way, by all means they should continue.

But cold canvassing is usually a time-waster. When we go door to door ringing doorbells, we ask similar questions of each home-owner. We ask if he wants to sell his home and if he knows of anyone else who might be thinking of selling his home. We have to ring scores of doorbells, which is very time-consuming, before we find a homeowner who gives us an affirmative answer. And then, we only have a listing lead, a lead that may prove worthless. The homeowner might answer that he will be selling his home in six months. It's a lead all right, but a poor one.

Psychology plays a major role in any sales effort. The adverse psychological effects of incessant pounding on one door after another, hour upon hour, day after day, can only corrupt ambition.

I expect my salesmen to have alert, active minds. I want them to look forward to each working day with anticipation. An office policy of door to door cold canvass solicitation for listings would make this next to impossible. I don't believe anyone can get out of bed with a smile on his face and hurry to the office bright and early, filled with pleasant anticipation, knowing that he will spend several hours ringing doorbells!

By devoting his efforts to expired multiple listings, "FOR SALE BY OWNER" signs, and newspaper ads, the industrious lister will have all the listing leads he needs. When he talks to these home-owners, he knows in advance that they want to sell. The lister's only job is convincing the property owners that they need professional help, and his help in particular.

The lister can thus spend all his time securing listings. He doesn't have to spend hours developing his leads as in cold canvass. Time is all important to every salesman. Let's not waste it trying to find prospects when bona fide listing prospects can be seen all over the city.

Cold Canvass Telephone. I believe in telephone solicitation for listings. However, I do not believe in a salesman spending hour upon hour dialing numbers from the reverse telephone directory.

You should make five phone calls each day for listing leads. If you do this on a regular basis, day in and day out, you will probably make more calls over a given time period than if you make many calls sporadically. I will discuss cold canvass telephone technique in detail in the next chapter.

Notices of Marriage and Divorce. This is a fine source of listings that requires more imagination and follow up, but will prove worth-while.

When a newly married couple is questioned regarding their housing plans, often they are delighted to learn that a modest down payment can really buy them a small home. It is usually not too difficult to find a home that can be purchased for a down payment that does not exceed the cash outlay required for the first and last month's advance rent on a leased apartment.

In a short time, this couple will be ready to purchase a more expensive home, after they sell the one they're living in.

In the case of divorce, large helpings of tact are mandatory. It is during trying times such as these that the professional real estate agent can be of great service. The economics of divorce often dictate the sale of a home.

News of Transfer or Promotion. When an article appears in the local newspaper telling of the transfer of an executive, this man should be contacted immediately. In addition to having an earnest need to sell his home, he might also have information concerning his replacement who will need to buy a home when he arrives.

When news of a man's promotion appears in print, many alert insurance salesmen make a point of contacting the man and advising him on the importance of increasing his insurance coverage in proportion to his increase in salary.

Why shouldn't the alert real estate agent also contact the newly promoted man? He will now be able to afford a more expensive home. Of course, he will have to sell his present home first!

Advertising. Many brokers recommend advertising as a method of securing listings. There are several forms of newspaper advertising for listings. "WE NEED LISTINGS" is the most obvious copy for such an ad. "FOR A FAST SALE, CONTACT ABC REALTY."

A real estate firm can advertise, "WE BUY EQUITIES." This will produce listing leads. The firm must be prepared to pay cash for an equity when called upon to do so. But many times the homeowner will decide to list his home for sale on the active market when the real estate agent gives him the "guarantee sale" figure.

In my office we have an "assured sales plan" whereby we advertise for equity purchases. We do secure a few listings this way but its primary advantage lies in the real estate investment benefits of such a program.

Some brokers use direct mail to produce listing leads. I have had a good deal of experience with direct mail solicitation. It is expensive. Considering the volume of leads produced, I believe direct mail solicitation for listings is a diseconomy. Institutional-type advertising for listings, such as billboards and property signs, will certainly produce listing leads over a period of time. But I am concerned with immediate results.

Very few general brokerage firms are so well financed, with such a surplus of spendable cash, that they can embark upon a long term campaign of institutional advertising, and such advertising requires time—lots of it!

Advertising for listings is, in my opinion, an alternative to aggressive sales effort. By its nature, the broker doing the advertising is waiting for the leads to come to him. It takes time, money, patience, and inertia! I believe in getting listings in bunches. It will never happen from advertising. Only "get up and go" creative selling will do the job.

Holding Homes Open. Contrary to popular belief, the principal benefit resulting from holding homes open is as a source of listing leads. Certainly homes are sold this way, but I am positive that salesmen earn more dollars from listing leads obtained in open houses than from sales commissions.

When I hold a home open, I always ask visitors the same question, "Do you have a home to sell before you can buy another?" I then offer to stop by their home to give them an appraisal. Many home owners make a hobby of touring open houses. An able listing specialist can turn them into sellers.

Other Sources. There are many additional sources of listing leads. None should be overlooked. Talk to everyone. Tell them you're in the real estate business. Give them your business card. Ask them to call you if they hear of someone who will be selling their home. You will get results.

Make listing contacts from the following:

(1) Tradesmen (delivery men, postmen).
(2) Attorneys.
(3) Bankers.
(4) Building and loan associations.
(5) Architects and civil engineers.
(6) Building contractors.
(7) Telephone canvassing areas of recent sales.
(8) Reports of future industrial or business development in an area.

Developing Leads
by Telephone

8

WE SHOULD LEARN
how to get listing leads by use of the telephone. Once you are inside

the home, the listing technique will be the same as the doorstep technique we shall discuss later. The telephone is an instrument to produce leads. A contract cannot be signed over the wires. That requires a personal confrontation. There are two main types of telephone procedure, expired multiple listing technique and the cold canvass technique.

Expired Multiple
Listing Technique

Only three basic questions are necessary to make the expired multiple listing technique work to perfection.

Before you call the seller indicated on the listing card, double check the listed expiration date to be certain that you are not usurping some other cooperating agent's rights.

I recommend waiting at least 24 hours after the listing has expired before calling. This is an extremely delicate point among real estate sales people throughout the country, as well it should be. The rules and regulations governing the solicitation of expired multiple listings set down by the local real estate boards should be respected and followed without reservation.

With the expired listing card beside the telephone so you can read it easily, dial the number of the seller. When he answers, introduce yourself. Be sure to speak clearly and slowly so the seller can understand you. Pronunciation is very important! As soon as the introduction is over, you are ready for question number one.

"Is your home still for sale?"

The seller doesn't know why you called. It is possible that you have a buyer sitting beside you while you are making the call. We want to keep this air of anticipation.

If the answer is no, find out if the home has been sold. If it has, congratulate him on his success. Explain that your records must have been in error for they did not show the sale. The homeowner is left with a good feeling toward real estate men in general.

However, if the answer is no, and the homeowner tells you that the home has not been sold, you must find out why the home is no longer for sale. In many cases the homeowner means that he has taken his home off the market temporarily to allow his wife to recover somewhat from the trials of maintaining the house constantly in inspection condition.

If this be the case, you have a first class listing prospect. If the homeowner answers yes, advising you that his home is still for sale, you ask question number two.

"I notice your home has gone off the market. Had you intended it to be withdrawn from sale?"

The seller still can't tell from this line of questioning whether you are looking for a listing or have a buyer standing by.

Many times the sellers will express surprise at learning their home is off the market. When they do, explain to them that your records indicate the agreement-to-sell-contract (don't use the word "listing") has terminated. This means that the hundreds of sales people who belong to your board's multiple listing service will withdraw the information card on the home from their files. They just assume the property is no longer for sale.

Now ask again, "Had you intended this?" Be very gentle. You can't afford to be abrupt. You must show the seller, with your voice alone, that you want to be of service, that you sincerely want to help him.

Many other times, the homeowner will reply that his home is still for sale. He didn't realize his contract has, in fact, expired. You must impress upon such a homeowner that when the contract termination date has passed, the property is considered no longer for sale regardless of the intent of the homeowner. You should not dwell on this point for an extended period. Go on to the final question.

"May I inspect your home at two o'clock this afternoon?"

You do not have to explain the purpose of your visit. If the seller says he is not going to sign another listing contract, you need not reply directly. "You would sell if I brought you an acceptable sales contract, wouldn't you?"

Once again, you needn't wait for a reply. "Will two o'clock this afternoon fit into your schedule?"

You'll get an affirmative reply, or at least another hour specified for your visit. Once you are in the home, you use the basic listing technique.

Cold Canvass
Telephone Technique

The other important telephone technique is the cold canvass method.

This is the only type of cold canvass solicitation I recommend to the lister. Only a few such calls should be made a day, but they should be made every day, at the same time of day, so that a habit pattern is established. I will discuss this more thoroughly in Chapter 19 dealing with a schedule for successful listing.

The easiest way to stimulate the interest of a stranger is to convey the impression that you need help, and that you are trying to help someone else at the same time. It's human nature to give aid to our fellow man when he's having problems.

In order that our listing approach doesn't ever take on an air of fabrication, we must go through our files, looking for a buying prospect who really does want to purchase a home in the particular neighborhood we've selected for our cold canvass telephone solicitation.

If we don't have such a prospect in our prospect list, perhaps one of the other salesmen in the office will be able to help. After all, they will be most anxious for you to secure a listing in an area where they can make a fast sale.

For example, let's say you want to get a new listing on Canyon Boulevard because properties sell very rapidly on that street. Search your prospect files, and select a buying prospect who would be interested in buying a home on that street if the price, terms, and condition of the home warranted it. Study the prospect card for a few minutes. Learn how much money the prospects have to put down in cash on a home. Determine their urgency for buying. Learn something about the size of their family. Now, go to the reverse telephone directory and select a telephone number on a house on Canyon Boulevard. Dial it.

When the homeowner answers, introduce yourself briefly. This is a departure from the technique used in telephoning an expired multiple listing. In the case of the expired multiple, the homeowner was conditioned to doing business with a real estate agent and had probably learned of the name of your office while his home was being offered for sale.

In the case of the cold canvass, the homeowner isn't conditioned to talking to a real estate man about anything, let alone selling his home. Therefore, we want to be very brief; just say enough to let him know what you are, not necessarily who you are. Say something like this:

"Hello, Mr. Jones, this is Thompson the real estate man." This lets him know he is speaking to a real estate agent. That's all he has to know at this time.

Continue your conversation in this vein. "Mr. Jones, I'm in trouble. I have a problem that is so serious that I've become desperate enough to call a perfect stranger to see if he could help me find a solution.

"You see, I have an awfully nice couple who are transferred down here from Redding and they've got to buy a home immediately. They have already sold their home in Redding and they've got $7,000 cash as a down payment.

"I've shown them homes all over the city and they just fell in love with the Canyon Boulevard area. I've done everything I know to find a home for sale there, but I keep running into blank walls.

"My buyers have three lovely children who would fit in perfectly with the other children in the neighborhood. Mr. Jones, would you by any chance know of anyone who is thinking of selling his home?"

The homeowner is immediately sympathetic with you because you are trying to help someone find a home. You have not solicited

Mr. Jones' listing, directly. You are merely helping a family when they need help. It is human nature for people to be helpful to others. If you approach it correctly, people will be more than helpful. You'll get suggestions as to whom to contact for a prospective listing.

"Well, I'm not thinking of selling myself, Mr. Realtor," is a common reply, "but I heard that the Murphys, they live across the street, have got to sell because Mr. Murphy has been transferred. I'd talk to them if I were you."

This is all you need from the telephone call. You have a wonderful lead. When you knock on the front door of the Murphy house later in the day, tell them that you heard Mr. Murphy was being transferred and they would be selling their home. Tell them about your buyer.

A variation of this technique is a bold, direct approach that works very well. When the homeowner answers his phone, introduce yourself briefly and then ask, "How soon are you going to be selling your home?"

It sounds as if someone had told you that the home would soon be for sale. The homeowner is surprised by the question. But more surprising, the lister will develop many listing leads this way. The conversation will take care of itself.

I prefer this latter technique since the "I need help" method is being overworked. The rest of the listing technique is easy. Finding the prospect was the work.

We shall discuss how to sell your firm, yourself, and the idea of using professional real estate help in the following chapters.

Listing Do's
and Don't's

9

MANY POTENTIALLY
fine listing salesmen defeat themselves before they ring the doorbell.

This chapter deals with things to do and not to do when listing. They are important. Concentrate upon them. Overlooking just one item may seem of no importance, but let me assure you, to neglect any one could easily mean the loss of a listing, or if repeated, the loss of the opportunity to learn to list successfully.

Do's
in Listing

Take Your Time. The first rule of professional listing is *take your time.* The lister should plan to take his time before he rings the doorbell.

I allot three hours for each listing call. Sometimes I have the listing in much less time. Other times I spend more than the three hours. Don't rush the homeowners. Be patient!

The listing should be taken on the first contact with husband and wife. To agree to delay the signing of the listing contract until another day is the "kiss of death" for the lister. Don't you do it!

Several years ago a salesman asked me to accompany him on a listing appointment. He was the finest real estate salesman I knew, but he was a poor lister.

I discovered his problem soon after we arrived at the home. He wanted to list like he sold. If the sellers did not indicate they were agreeing with his remarks within 15 minutes, he would immediately break off the conversation and leave. He had no patience. I pointed this out to him and he began spending more time with homeowners. His listing success grew overnight.

Time had been the culprit. Remember. Take your time.

Speak Slowly. When speaking, you should speak slowly, very slowly. This commands attention. Your thoughts must be quick. You should not treat yourself to the luxury of long pauses between sentences, but the speech should be slow.

People tend to disbelieve others who speak rapidly. Precise speech is interesting. Precise speech is easily understood. You should enunciate clearly, with careful pronunciation of words. A clipped diction is more thought-arresting than a rapid, slurred jumble of words.

When speaking, you should use words that command attention. Each salesman can easily add a few such words to his vocabulary. Words such as *dignity, substantial, capricious, professional, equate, gracious,* are attention-getting.

When making a point that requires an acceptance of stated fact, say, "It's accurate," and then be quiet. "What I say is accurate. You can depend upon it."

Wait until the prospective seller speaks. You can readily determine if the point you were making was well taken.

Use a Person's Name. You should call a person by name. While in the Army, I was an instructor at the Security Agency School in Massachusetts. It was there I learned the power of using a person's name.

Each time you call a person by his name, you short circuit his mind. No matter what he is saying, no matter how emotional the discussion, for a fraction of a second his thought pattern is broken. This gives you an advantage.

I also learned that when you ask questions, you control the conversation. When someone asks you a question, he is in momentary control of the conversation. The successful salesman has to control the conversation in order to lead the thought processes of the seller.

"Mr. Mayberry, let me ask you this." That sentence has sales magic in it. It can mesmerize. It can lead to riches.

Of course, anything can be overdone. You can't call a man by his name every other sentence, and you can't keep asking questions. Use moderation.

Always Agree. Don't disagree with a seller. Agree, and then suggest another approach. A seller won't sign a listing contract if he feels you're not on his side. No matter what develops, don't get into any arguments. If the seller makes a statement that you don't agree with, say, "Of course, but let me ask you this." Your question can steer him right back on the path you want him to follow.

Be Friendly. The final "DO" is so simple it can be overlooked all too easily. Be friendly. A sincerely friendly nature is contagious. A smile infects like a firm handshake. If a man likes you, and keeps liking you, you're a long way toward getting his signature. Until you get that signature, be persistent, but gentle.

Don't's
in Listing

Don't Carry a Briefcase. When walking up to a front door, don't carry a briefcase. Consider the housewife who is going to answer the doorbell. She expects the caller to be her next door neighbor returning a cup of sugar.

She does not want to be suddenly confronted by a door to door salesman or, for that matter, anyone who will put her on the defensive. To ask a person to buy something, or to ask them something that requires thought for an answer, will put that person instantly on the defensive.

A briefcase makes the listing agent look like a peddler. He does not look like a professional. You can carry all the forms that are required in your coat pocket or purse.

The moment the housewife opens the front door and sees a gentleman with a briefcase, she begins forming her defensive tactics. You would do well to turn on your heel and leave. You would have a slim chance of convincing her you weren't trying to sell something. A briefcase is surplus equipment to the successful lister.

Don't Call After Dark. Don't ring a doorbell after dark. There is always a measure of resistance to a stranger standing at your door. A stranger standing at your door in darkness magnifies that resistance many times. Let's put everything we can in our favor!

Don't Say "Listing." When trying to secure a listing, don't mention the word "listing." That single word has raised more hackles on the backs of more FOR SALE BY OWNERS than any other word.

We want to keep the homeowner off balance. Until the lister mentions listing, the homeowner isn't quite sure what the agent has in mind. Don't use the word "deal" when speaking to a homeowner. It has an unpleasant connotation.

Don't Tout Your Firm. Don't talk about your firm initially. This is one of the most common mistakes real estate salesmen make in the pursuit of listings.

They knock on the door, introduce themselves, and start bragging about the sales history of their firms. At that point in the homeowner-salesman relationship, listing is farthest from the seller's mind. He does not care to hear tales about real estate firms. He does not care to hear about you! Can you really blame him?

The only way the salesman is going to hold the attention of the homeowner is to quickly begin asking questions—questions whose answers present no challenge to the seller's mental agility, questions whose answers are of definite interest to the seller. The story about your office comes later.

Don't talk about competitive real estate firms ever. There's a wealth of truth in the adage, "A knock is a boost."

Don't Promise Advertising. Don't promise advertising to a seller. Many times sellers ask if the agent will advertise his property if they give him the listing.

Remember, you should consider yourself a professional. When you go to a doctor for some ailment, you are prepared to put your health in his hands without reservation. You expect the doctor to prescribe a course of action for you. You wouldn't think of telling the doctor what he should prescribe for you.

You are the person who does the prescribing, not the seller! If this was not so, there would be little need for real estate agents. The seller actually wants to do business with a professional, a person who will explain to him in detail, if necessary, just what will be done to sell his home. But the methods of creating sales activity must come from you.

When you are asked if you are going to advertise the home, you should answer as follows:

Mr. Mayberry, I cannot guarantee advertising on your home. I am not the person who selects which homes my firm will advertise.

Real estate firms employ three different types of advertising policy. They advertise to sell a specific home, they advertise to pacify a seller, or they advertise for customers.

An intensive survey among leading real estate firms throughout the country showed that only one house out of 27 is sold from an advertisement. That's a pretty poor ratio.

It's hard to believe, but some firms actually do advertise homes just to keep the sellers happy. They are letting the sellers dictate sales policy to them. I know you wouldn't want to do business with that kind of firm. You wouldn't need professional help if you knew all the advertising answers.

The most successful real estate offices advertise for customers. They advertise homes that are the most "advertiseable." That's an awkward word, I know, but it means the home has features that will cause the readers to call for more information. Not all homes have these features.

When the potential buyer comes to our office, we qualify him to learn of his financial status and to determine more accurately the type of home he will buy.

Then we show him several homes that fit these needs. Many times the buyer never sees the home that was advertised. The difference is that we sell many more homes following this policy than if we pursued one of the others.

Rest assured, Mr. Mayberry, that my firm will continually advertise properties that will bring us buyers who are interested in your type of home.

Don't Promise to Sell. Another important *don't:* Don't promise a homeowner that you can sell his home. Explain again that homes are purchased in great measure on emotion. It is next to impossible to predict a stranger's emotional reaction to any particular home. Your job is to assay this from your experience, but, at best, it is only a well calculated guess.

Explain that your main job is to cause the home to be sold. You are competing with all the salesmen on your multiple listing service. The odds are against you, but you'll do your best. You make more money if you sell the home yourself, and don't have to share the commission with another salesman, but first of all, you want the home to sell. That's your job, and you're good at it!

Don't Name a Sales Price. Don't name a specific price that the home will sell for. We don't have to belabor this point. It is self-explanatory.

Don't Use Slang. Don't use slang or poor grammar. There is nothing that will destroy the professional image more rapidly than disregarding this advice.

Don't be careless about your appearance. Wear a suit and tie. In my area, it gets up to 120 degrees in the summer, but every one of my salesmen wears a suit and tie, and they've made money because of it. A neurosurgeon receiving patients in a sport shirt wouldn't make a very favorable impression on the worried patient.

Get a haircut weekly, and a shoe shine while you're at it. If you're going to be professional, you'll have to look professional!

Don't Smoke. This last one is tough for many. Don't smoke unless the homeowner does so first. I have seen sellers deeply offended, usually for religious reasons, when an unthinking salesman lit a cigarette in their home.

One of the first things I look for when I enter a strange home is ashtrays. The absence of them tells a story in itself. But even if you see an ashtray, ask if you can smoke. It is important. Don't neglect it.

Why Home-
Owners Don't List

10

BEFORE WE CAN DE-
velop a formula for listing, we should first have a good idea of why

[89]

the homeowner didn't come to us for help in the first place. A study of these listing obstacles will be most rewarding.

There are four principal obstacles the professional lister has to overcome as regards a seller's resistance to signing a listing contract. In this chapter we shall only point them out. In the following chapters we will learn how to overcome them.

Save the Commission

Number one, the homeowner tries to sell his home by himself in order to save the real estate commission. He has heard of others selling their homes themselves. It is only logical, so it seems, to give it a try himself. After all, he worked awfully hard for his money!

Fear of Salesmen

Number two, the average homeowner is afraid of salesmen in general. Perhaps it could be more accurately expressed by saying the average person is uncomfortable when confronted by a salesman.

Consider for a moment how you feel when you walk past a used car lot. I mean when you haven't been thinking about buying a car. You're just walking down the street and suddenly you look up and see a used car that catches your fancy.

You'd kind of like to take a look under the hood, or sit behind the wheel, but you spot the salesman approaching from the other side of the lot. He'd seen the spark of interest flash across your face. He'd be waiting for you beside the car.

So you keep on walking along the sidewalk. If that salesman hadn't been there, you might have had time to kick a tire or two. But you weren't conditioned to talking to a salesman so you went on your way.

I enjoy browsing through department stores with no particular purchase in mind. I can remember on one such excursion wandering into the heavy appliance department to look at an attractive display of refrigerators.

I was having a wonderful time looking through a large, new model. It seemed to have scores of new gadgets inside. I can clearly remember just beginning to examine the ice cube maker when I spotted the salesman peeking at me through the crack in the door. My pleasurable excursion ended abruptly. It's not that I feared the salesman as a person. It's just that I didn't want to have to begin concocting defenses to his sales pitches. I wasn't prepared to think about refrigerators in earnest.

This is an important point. Conditioning a prospect's mind is mandatory!

Let's go back to the used car lot. If you had been thinking about buying a car for some time and had finally decided to go down to the lot to look them over, you would have welcomed the salesman. You would need him to answer your questions. You would have been conditioned to dealing with a salesman of automobiles.

In the department store example, if I had been thinking of buying a refrigerator, I would have been pleased to find a salesman peering over my shoulder. Conditioning the mind is all important!

If you were walking down the street with a friend one fine afternoon, and the friend suddenly led you into a movie theater, sat you down, and told you you were going to watch the picture, you would not enjoy the movie nearly as much as if you had planned to see the very same movie and had thought about it, even if just for a few minutes, before making your decision to buy a ticket.

The reason for this is conditioning. You had conditioned your mind to watching a movie. You had certainly expected to enjoy yourself. You had, in fact, presold yourself on the movie. This is the purpose of the advertising about the picture, to precondition your mind.

If we, as professionals in the listing business, can recognize the importance of this type of presales conditioning, we will be much better prepared to meet success in our chosen profession.

We, as real estate salesmen knocking on a prospective seller's door, have to expect to meet an unconditioned mind as regards signing a listing contract. We, therefore, must adopt a strategy that will overcome this basic stumbling block. This, we shall learn to do.

The Confident
Seller

The third major obstacle you must overcome is the average seller's inherent confidence in his own ability to sell his home without help from anyone.

He feels a challenge in selling his home. He is the master of his household, so he thinks! He doesn't need help from anyone and he has probably told his wife, his neighbors, and all his friends the same thing. We, as listers, are then going to have to give this man an excuse for signing a contract with us.

This is a creature practically drowning in his own false pride. Unless we can show him how he can gracefully explain away his sudden reversal of policy, we will not get the listing. The most successful way of overcoming this feeling of righteous self-assurance is to shatter the seller's confidence in his knowledge of real estate.

After all, the reason he felt so all fired bright in the first place is because he pictures the average real estate salesman as having a small brain and expending the absolute minimum of energy on work. He thinks that once he signs a listing, a buyer will miraculously appear from the bushes and the salesman will get a fat commission check for no work at all. We will soon learn how to destroy this image once and for all.

Seller's
Uncertainty

The fourth, and final, major obstacle we will have to face is the homeowner's uncertainty about the mechanics of selling through an agent.

I have worked for hours with apparently stubborn sellers, trying everything I knew to get their signatures on a contract. I had overcome every objection they offered to me. They agreed that my answers were logical. They accepted them as fact. Still, they wouldn't sign.

Many times the seller will not tell you the true reason he isn't grabbing for your pen. The listing agent has to search for the truth. You have to diagnose.

This final major block, seller's uncertainty, has proved, time and again, to be the villain. The seller thinks that once he signs the listing contract, his home will be invaded, day and night, by rude, boisterous salesmen and buyers. If we can eliminate these fears, he will sign right now!

I remember a widow to whom I was talking express a deathly fear of real estate salesmen. It seems that several years earlier, a house next door to her own was for sale. The owners had already moved to another city.

One morning the lady was standing in front of her house watering the lawn when she saw a real estate man park his car in front of the neighboring house and walk up to the front door. Apparently he forgot his lockbox key and seeing the house vacant and a window conveniently open, he proceeded to enter the house through the window.

The widow did not understand. From that moment on, she lived with the impression that once a house was for sale, the real estate people would do everything but come down the chimney!

This seems ridiculous to those of us in the industry, but similar feelings exist all over the country. We must be sure to allay these fears. A few words of careful explanation and we've got the listing. I make certain I tell the homeowners exactly what to expect once they have let me go to work for them.

Here we have, then, the four obstacles we, as listers, must overcome.

With the fund of information we have gained to this point, we are now well prepared to deal directly with a seller.

We are going out together to knock on his door and get a listing. We have found a home in a desirable neighborhood that sports an awkwardly constructed "FOR SALE BY OWNER" sign on its front lawn. It's a bright, sunny day, eleven o'clock in the morning.

Let's park our car, which has been freshly washed, at the curb. Our briefcase can stay on the back seat. Just in case the homeowner is breathlessly waiting for a real estate man to knock on his door so he can give him a listing (I've had this happen), I have an exclusive listing contract folded neatly in the breast pocket of my suit.

Remember now, look professional, feel professional, be professional.

There's the doorbell. Push it, and start smiling.

Ask Ten
Magic Questions

11

NO SUBJECT HAS AT-
tracted as much comment, both pro and con, among sales managers

across the nation, as the so called "canned" or prepared sales talk.

In the large, volume sales organizations such as insurance companies, small appliance companies, encyclopedia companies and the like, the prepared sales talk is the very foundation of their success.

The Prepared
Sales Talk

When a new salesman goes to work for one of the nation's leading encyclopedia companies, he is taken into a private room and given a prepared sales talk to memorize *word for word*.

After several days, he has memorized the entire talk. He is then assigned a territory and sent out to begin knocking on doors.

The encyclopedia company has had such extensive experience in this art that they can predict to the week when that same salesman will return to the office a dejected man.

"Money's gettin' awful tight," he complains. "People just aren't interested in encyclopedias anymore. Never met so many rude housewives. You sure gave me a lousy territory."

Without great concern, the salesman is taken back into the private room and asked to recite his sales talk. He can't remember how it starts. He has substituted an introduction he felt would be better. He has forgotten half of the points. The points that he remembers are not in correct order. In short, the salesman has improvised to such an extent that the whole talk might as well be assigned to the rubbish heap.

He is then given another copy of the sales talk and asked to memorize it. When he does, he goes back to his territory and suddenly the housewives become more friendly, money becomes more readily committed and the territory takes on a new and fresher bloom.

That is the power of the canned sales talk. It works, it gets predictable results, it is readily controlled. I believe that a modified, prepared sales talk should be used in listing. You should use your own words, but you should not improvise on the points or their order of use.

The Magic
Questions

I have ten questions that I always ask a seller when I want to get his listing. I never vary the order of the questions. I never leave out a question. By the time the homeowner has answered all of the questions, I have him conditioned to such a point that getting him to sign the contract is just a formality.

The answers to the ten questions give me all the information about the seller I need to know in order to calculate my method of closing with assurance of success. I know what the seller wants to hear. In addition, I know in advance what I am going to say when the door opens. I'm not going to stand there and take my cues from the homeowner. I'm going to control the conversation.

For the purpose of this chapter, let us assume that we are ringing a doorbell in the morning of a typical working day. We can assume the husband is not at home. He is probably at his job. Therefore, we want this first contact with the FOR SALE BY OWNER seller to accomplish two goals: let the housewife get to know us, and give us the answers to our questions so we will know how to approach the husband later that evening.

Be sure not to begin selling the housewife on listing with your firm if the husband is not home. It takes two signatures on a listing contract. If you have spent a considerable amount of time explaining some of your principal sales points, the wife will become bored when you go over the same points later in the evening with her husband. No matter what, you have to hold the attention of your subjects.

As soon as the housewife opens the door, smile broadly, introduce yourself, name your real estate firm and hand your business card to her. If she is standing behind a screen door, ask her if she won't please take the card. If you suggest people do something for you, and you do it properly, they will usually comply.

This is actually the first step in establishing a habit pattern of compliance with your wishes. Get the homeowner to take your business card.

Be certain not to apologize for disturbing her, and don't apologize for being from a real estate firm. You are there to help her. She needs professional advice. She needs you, Mr. Lister!

When you are standing there with your card in your hand, look like you're proud of what you're doing. As soon as she has your business card, you ask question number one in this manner:

1. "I noticed a 'FOR SALE' sign on your front lawn. *How much are you asking?*"

If she counters with the comment that they are selling themselves, say, "I understand that, but you would consider an offer if I brought you one, wouldn't you?"

Now you have piqued her curiosity. Most times, however, you will get a direct answer to a direct question. If she tells you the price and then advises you that they are not going to seek realtor help, say, "I don't blame you. I'd save that commission too if I were you."

You are being pleasant. You have taken the first step toward overcoming the homeowner's basic antagonism toward salesmen. In addition, you have a most valuable piece of information about the prospective listing.

Now keep the questions coming. Remember, when you are asking questions, you are in command of the conversation. You must ask questions that are both interesting to the homeowner and easy for her to answer. The questions cannot require much thought.

2. *"Have you had any offers?"*

If the answer is yes, ask if they were government-insured offers or conventional financing. She probably won't know the answer. Whether she does or not, regardless of the answer, say, "I'm sorry none of the offers were acceptable to you. I know how frustrating it can be to sell a home. My wife tells me it's one of the toughest jobs a housewife has. She lives in mortal fear of the day I come home and announce we're going to sell the house. In this business, we sell more often than others."

Certainly you don't have to use these exact words. Just be friendly. Be interested in your prospect. If the housewife says she has had no offers, don't comment at all. It could prove embarrassing to the seller and you stand a good chance of alienating her.

Go immediately to the next question.

3. "How long have you had your home on the market?"

If the answer to the previous question was that they had received no offers, and she now tells you they have had their home on the market a considerable period of time, the point is clear enough to her. For goodness sake, don't belabor it.

The answer to this question also has another significance. It tells you if the home is becoming "ripe" for an easy listing. Most FOR SALE BY OWNERS will list their homes more easily after they have tried three or four weeks themselves. This is something to watch for.

Next question.

4. "Have you been advertising in the newspaper?"

If the answer is no, you have a hint that the sellers aren't taking their own sales efforts too seriously.

Many people feel they just have to put up a "FOR SALE" sign for a week or two in case a buyer should happen along and take their home away from them. They can hardly wait for the real estate agent to appear on the scene and give them enough sound reasons for acquiring professional help so that they can sign a listing contract and be done with it.

If the answer to this question is yes, ask what paper they're using. No matter which paper is mentioned, praise her on her choice. Ask who writes the ads, she or her husband. You're giving her a perfect opportunity to strut. How we all adore this! A compliment doesn't really hurt, and it can accomplish so much.

The next question.

5. "Have you seen our ads?"

If the housewife answers no, we can assume she hasn't been following the classified pages at all. This can be dangerous. It usually means she doesn't care what the real estate firms are doing, she's going to do it her way or else! However, it can merely signify a total lack of interest in what the professionals are doing.

This is less common, but it can show that she isn't planning a long holdout; she's more like the seller we just mentioned. She thought she ought to give it a try.

If the answer to this question is yes, she has seen your firm's ads in the paper, your sailing is going to be easier. This means she is comparing her ad to the pro's. She has noticed your ads. She can easily detect their professional tone. Any serious comparison of the two would be odious.

The fact that she has seen your firm's ads also means that the stature, the image of your firm, has been impressed upon her mind.

You're making progress. If you stopped right now and reflected upon how much you have learned about the sellers in a short time, with half of the ten questions asked and answered, you would be pleasantly surprised.

6. *"May I see the inside of your home?"*

Until now, you have been standing at the front door. "The front yard looks so nice, I'd sure like to take a quick look inside."

She'll probably parry this suggestion, saying the beds aren't made or the dishes are still in the sink.

That's easy. "Don't worry about that," you assure her, "I'll just take a minute. I'd like to get an idea of the floor plan." Now move toward the entry hall. She will let you in.

You haven't mentioned the word "listing," or even faintly suggested that she let you sell her home for her. For all she knows, you have an anxious buyer with a wallet full of money waiting around the corner, beside himself with anticipation of giving it all to her!

Fear not, she'll quickly welcome you.

7. *"Why are you selling?"*

Just like in the mystery novels, always look for the motive. Either her husband has been transferred or they have purchased another home or one of the children is allergic to some local grasses or perhaps they just thought they'd see how much they could get for their house. If this be the case, this last supposition, they really aren't bona fide sellers at all. They're merely suspects.

But in the other cases, there is true urgency. When you determine the reason for selling, you can easily determine what kind of ammunition to load into your big guns when you return later that evening, when the husband is home, to sign up the listing contract.

For example, if she says her husband has been transferred, find out where he has been transferred to. This shows her you're interested in the new job, but what it doesn't show her, and what you want from this question, is to know just how far away the new job is. If it's too far for him to commute easily every night, you can bet your last dollar that they will seek professional help very soon.

When you have learned where the family is moving, ask when her husband has to report for his new job. That's all the research we'll do on this point. But when you're talking to the husband, you can explain to him just how long it takes to close an escrow even with highly skilled persons working at top speed. A government-insured contract could require 90 days or more in escrow before the sellers received their check.

When this is made clear to the FOR SALE BY OWNER, his plans of "giving it a try himself for awhile" will quickly change.

8. *"Do you have any loan commitments?"*

This question is loaded to the brim! Usually the answer is no. Sometimes the homeowner will reply that they have an FHA or a GI appraisal. If so, ask what the appraisal figures are.

If the answer is no, they have no loan commitments, you make a mental note to stress the importance of getting loan commitments in advance of bringing buyers through the home. This will be a strong selling point for the husband.

9. *"Do you have deposit receipts and promissory notes?"*

If the answer is yes, you can expect a more difficult task before you. The seller has gone to the trouble of getting the necessary forms from a title company. They probably don't know what to do with the forms, but their very presence in the home makes the sellers feel that they are fulfilling their prideful obligations to themselves to try it alone for a bit.

Most of the time the answer to this question will be no. In that case, it is useful to mention that you will bring some of the blank forms by and explain their use to her husband.

This makes the lister appear to be helpful. The housewife makes her own mental note to give you a call when they finally get ready to sign a listing.

Read that last sentence again! You read it and accepted it as being true, because it was true. ". . . when they finally get ready to sign a listing."

The homeowner really, down deep inside, expects to sign a listing contract with a real estate agent. Your only task is to speed the time of compliance to today.

Once again I should point out the true significance of this apparently foolhardy offer to bring fodder to the "enemy's horses." Returning with a few deposit receipt forms gives you a perfect entry, that of the helpful friend. The sellers just couldn't send you away without giving you a few moments of their valuable time. That's all you need!

Offer to show the sellers how to fill in the deposit receipt form. Offer to fill in a sample promissory note. You can even throw in the FHA amendment forms, the standard termite clauses, and as many other confusing bits of real estate functionalism as you consider necessary to thoroughly confuse the seller.

When the FOR SALE BY OWNER confesses that they have no deposit receipts or promissory note forms in the house, they are giving evidence of their willingness to list. If they intended to fight it out themselves, they would have the forms stacked beside the front door.

10. "Will your husband be home at 6 PM?"

You want to return when they are both at home. That's when you will go into your sales presentation. That's when you're going to get the listing contract signed.

Don't phrase this last question as follows: "When will your husband be home?"

See the difference? You're asking the seller to think, to remember if her husband had any late appointments that evening, to make a conclusion as to when he would be home. You're making it too easy for her to destroy everything you've done 'til then, to lay waste all the information you have gained. She could easily reply that he won't be home until very late and he will be tired.

"Will your husband be home at 6 PM?" The answer is either yes or no. She might launch into a bit of an explanation, but that is easily controlled.

"Does your husband eat dinner with the children every evening? I'll bet that's around six o'clock, isn't it?"

Remember this. Put words into your clients' mouths. They will put dollars into your pockets.

After you have discovered when the husband will arrive home from work, don't announce that you will be coming back at that time. The wife, trying to protect her work-weary spouse from the clutches of a predatory salesman, will always ask you not to return that evening. She'll advise you to call on the weekend for an appointment. Don't put yourself in the position of being turned down!

You've got the information you need. The expert salesman knows when to leave. You're becoming an expert most rapidly, so leave.

Thank the lady for her graciousness. Remind her that if she ever has any questions whatsoever regarding real estate, you are as near as her phone and you would consider it a personal favor to be able to help her at any time.

You can't kill 'em with kindness, but you surely can wow 'em with loads and loads of courtesy.

When you next ring that lady's doorbell, she will greet you as a friend. You have not asked her to sign anything. You have not produced any legal looking forms and thrust them under her nose. You have not insulted her for trying to sell her home herself. You have complimented her on the appearance of her home. You have offered help and advice. You have only asked a few questions, about things she was interested in discussing.

You have departed as friends.

Do you really know what you just were? You were the first half of a sophisticated, professional lister. You have that poor, defenseless couple "set up" for a signing! You know their weaknesses. You know their strength. You know what kind of bullets to put in your listing gun. You even know exactly where to aim it.

How unfair! This approach to selling, and listing is real selling, takes almost all of the sport out of it. The outcome is preordained. You know you're going to get the listing. The only question that remains unanswered is just how long will it take. It will be longer than ten minutes but less than three hours.

Somewhere in that tolerance of time you will put several hundred dollars, perhaps thousands, in your pocket.

I have listed the ten Magic Questions in order for easy assimilation. Study them.

1. How much are you asking?
2. Have you had any offers?
3. How long has your home been on the market?
4. Have you been advertising in the newspaper?
5. Have you seen our ads?
6. May I see the inside of your home?
7. Why are you selling?
8. Do you have any loan commitments?
9. Do you have deposit receipts and promissory notes?
10. Will your husband be home at 6 PM?

Don't be too concerned about the detail of the dialogue offered in this chapter. The ten Magic Questions are the key to all listing success. If you have memorized the questions and ask them in order, your conversation with the homeowner will take care of itself. Never again will you be unsure of yourself when you ring a doorbell.

Let's learn some more. We want to have as great an advantage as possible.

Developing a
Listing Dialogue

12

IT MAKES NO DIF-
ference whether we have arrived this evening at the prospective

seller's home as the result of following a FOR SALE BY OWNER sign and our 10 question technique, a telephone conversation following a lead proffered by an expired multiple listing card, the cold canvass telephone technique, or any other source, the procedures we use from here on are the same.

They will vary only slightly as the dialogue between homeowner and lister develops. A listing letter would certainly pave the way for us. It would help project our image as professionals.

As we develop our listing dialogue, we must overcome the 4 major obstacles mentioned in Chapter 10 (1—save the 6% commission, 2—fear of salesmen in general, 3—the self-confident seller, 4—the uncertainty of listing mechanics).

Setting
the Scene

The husband is home now, so we can use our full listing dialogue. Let's assume it is six o'clock in the evening. The homeowners are Mr. and Mrs. Fred Miller. You hold several deposit receipts, promissory note forms, and FHA amendment forms in your hand.

Ring the doorbell. Mrs. Miller comes to the door and recognizes you from earlier in the day. You are not a stranger. You were the "friendly" real estate salesman. She has probably mentioned your previous visit to her husband already, so that both of them are somewhat conditioned to your presence.

Be very cordial when you meet Mr. Miller. Be sure to introduce yourself to him because Mrs. Miller might not remember your name, or your firm, exactly. It saves her from a minor embarrassment. Give him a business card.

"Mr. Miller," you begin, "I see you are interested in selling your home. I would like to help you. I've brought some real estate forms for you to use when you get a buyer. I know you can use them. I would like to show you a few things about filling them out."

Everyone is irritated by a salesman who does not come to the point. Keep the conversation moving.

"May I sit down a moment?" Walk on into the living room and

take a seat. It would be disastrous to remain standing in the entrance hall. You would be uncomfortable, and Mr. and Mrs. Miller would be anxious for you to take your leave.

At this time, the homeowner might counter with the first of his two or three stock defenses. Each seller has a few objections to signing a listing contract that seemed to work with all the real estate salesmen so far. You're going to be the exception.

Being a successful salesman is like being a successful doctor. Both must be expert diagnosticians. The professional lister has to quickly find just what objections the particular seller is going to use, and what the reasons are for these objections. As soon as you have learned this, you can counter the objections and begin writing the listing contract.

"We thought that we'd try ourselves for a while, but we'll give you a call when we get ready to list."

I have heard this objection more than any other. It works with most real estate salesmen. I find that very sad, but very true.

An entire family is depending on the salesman for a living; they love him and have worlds of confidence in his ability, yet this same salesman allows himself to be verbally browbeaten with an ineffectual objection, and accepts defeat.

Each salesman should realize that, to his family, he is like a field marshall on the battlefield. He has the authority to declare victory or defeat, not only for himself, but for his entire family.

Selling is friendly, but serious, verbal combat. We don't want to lose. There is really no reason why we should lose. We want to get a signature on a listing contract. The wonderful thing about the real estate business is that a signature on a contract is as advantageous to the signatory's as it is to the salesman's family.

That is why real estate, practiced properly, is a profession. The professional real estate agent gives accurate, detailed information in the spirit of service.

Back to our listing adventure.

Start talking! Don't wait for Mr. Miller to pose an objection. If an objection is raised, answer it and then continue on with your predetermined dialogue.

"Mr. Miller, I don't blame you for trying to sell your home yourself. If I were in your position and could sell my house and save the commission, I would do it. I know you work awfully hard for your money, and the real estate commission isn't exactly peanuts!"

You've thrown him off balance. You must remember always to agree, never argue, never disagree. Agree, and then offer an explanation.

Overcome
Commission Obstacle

"Commission is a nebulous thing, Mr. Miller, when you consider how much money you're asking someone to pay for your home.

"Regardless of whether you are selling by yourself or with the help of a real estate firm, buyers usually figure the asking price includes a commission. They expect it. FHA and GI appraisers, bank and insurance company appraisers, all consider their fair market appraisal to include a commission. Buyers know this! They will usually offer at least 6% less than your asking price.

"That's the reason folks who try to sell themselves get such low offers. If they do eventually get an offer, and the odds are against them, it will be low. I bet you'll agree with me, Mr. Miller, that you've attracted mostly lookers, or investment seekers, to inspect your home.

"Do you know why this is so? Speculators think that because you don't have professional real estate help, they will be able to take advantage of your lack of specific real estate knowledge. Many times they are successful. I want you to know this so you'll be prepared when the next buyer comes along.

"The majority of home buyers will definitely not buy direct from an owner. There are sound reasons for this. The most important one is value. Very few people outside my industry really know the true market value of any particular home.

"They know that when they buy through a real estate agent, they have a professional advising them of comparative values.

"Consider, Mr. Miller, if you were suddenly transferred to, say, Peoria, Illinois. You don't know a thing about the city. You don't know anything about the schools, or the various neighborhoods, or the relative prices of homes.

"Would you begin driving up one street and down the other looking for homes for sale by their owners? Would you seek out FOR SALE BY OWNER ads in the newspapers, or would you find a responsible real estate firm and ask them to help you?

"The answer is easy. You know you just wouldn't depend upon what an owner told you about their home and their asking price without getting professional help to verify the statements. A home is too expensive an investment. It's too permanent. It's not like buying something through a classified ad in the newspaper for $25.

"The majority of people agree with you 100%, Mr. Miller, for they, also, would seek professional help. But by trying to sell your home yourself, you are temporarily acting in a fashion that fosters overtones of distrust for you as an individual.

"Other strangers who are looking for a home can't know you like I know you. They can't know that you are an honest man. When they see your sign in your front lawn, or read your ad in the paper, they immediately store a tiny bit of information in their subconscious that says, 'be careful of that man, he bears watching.' They know you only have one home to sell. You would react exactly the same way yourself."

You're getting a little rough with the prospective seller so take it easy. Remember to speak slowly, clearly, and be friendly. Be gentle. The information you are telling the homeowner can stand on its own feet.

You continue. "Mr. Miller, the man who buys a home not only expects a commission to be included in the sales price, but is actually very concerned and interested that it be there.

"He is willing to pay for professional help. He is going to sign his name to a mortgage obligating him to pay many thousands of dollars over many years in the future. He wants protection. The best protection he can have is professional advice from a person knowledgeable in real estate values. That's me!

"When you consider the commission being a small percentage

of the total sales price, and spread the amount of the commission over the term of the new loan that the buyer is going to put on the home, his monthly contribution to paying off that commission will be negligible.

"Only one out of 500 homeowners sell their homes successfully themselves. I stress the word 'successfully.' A recent survey showed that of all the homeowners who sold their homes themselves, four out of six of these sellers would have netted more money if they had sold through a real estate firm.

"Buyers will pay more money for a home when they buy through a responsible real estate agency.

"Another point, Mr. Miller, that you should consider. When you attempt to sell your home without professional help, you're asking your wife to open her door to any stranger who rings the doorbell. You have no way of knowing who might call on a newspaper advertisement or who might knock on your door. Mrs. Miller can't qualify them in advance. She is home alone much of the day. There are some strange people who follow FOR SALE BY OWNER ads. Some are just curious. Some like to look at furniture. Others are just lonely and like to talk. Very seldom do you find a qualified buyer.

"Customers of ours who have let us sell their homes for them tell us that one reason they wanted professional help in selling was that they just couldn't put up with the constant interruptions they had when they tried by themselves. We screen prospective buyers for you as to financial ability and desire, and then show your home only by advance appointment. Inconvenience is held to a minimum."

As our listing presentation develops, you can see that we are giving sound reasons for listing, and we are giving them in logical order.

Note that in our dialogue we alternate our points of interest from husband to wife and back to husband. We want to keep their mutual interest. We should not talk only to the husband. It takes two signatures on a listing contract!

Price and commission are of interest to the husband. Being

strangers in a city appeals to the wife. The relative costs of professional help is of interest to the husband, as are the survey figures. The strangers in the house information, and the constant interruptions discussion, interest the wife.

You continue. Watch your use of language. You are a professional. It is easy to become so carried away with talk that the skill of presentation becomes lost in a hurried slur of words.

Pause between the various points. Let the homeowners absorb their meaning fully. They will make comments along the way. You are being interesting. In order to continue to be, in order to continue to hold their attention, you must use your language skillfully. To this point, you have successfully countered the commission obstacle.

Overcome
Obstacle of Fear

You have also overcome the obstacle of instinctive fear of sales people. You have shown, through your choice of words, your pleasantly modulated voice, your bearing, your friendly nature, that you are indeed a gracious person. You are not a high pressure sales person.

Objection number three is about to be met. You must point out the seller's lack of essential knowledge of all things pertaining to real estate. You must upset the seller's confidence in himself. You have already overcome this obstacle as far as Mrs. Miller is concerned by mentioning the "strangers in the house." But Mr. Miller is our primary target. It is usually the man of the house who feels the "do-it-yourself" urge.

"Mr. Miller, real estate salesmen buy homes for themselves. Let's say I decided to buy your home. I want to purchase on an FHA basis. How many points would you have to pay?"

Wait for his answer. Let him think a moment. No matter what his answer regarding the number of points, tell him he is wrong! It happens to be true. Explain that the number of points that will be charged a seller cannot be determined in advance with absolute certainty. The precise number of points is determined at the time the escrow closes, which could be months from the time the sales contract was written, and even then the point charges vary according to the credit of the buyer and the amount of his cash down payment.

"No, Mr. Miller," you advise him, "no one can forecast point charges with precision." You have cracked his confidence. You had better keep at it.

"Do you know how much I could borrow on an FHA basis, Mr. Miller? There is a definite loan-to-value ratio the FHA prescribes for loans. It's not hard to remember.

"The FHA will insure a lender against loss for 97% of the first $25,000 of appraised value, 90% of the next $10,000, and 80% of the balance to a maximum of $45,000.

"Unless, of course, the home is less than one year old and it was not constructed under FHA specifications. Then they will insure 90% of what the loan would have been if it was a regular FHA loan."

This sounds confusing. I intend that it should. We are trying to give Mr. Miller a realistic idea of the knowledge necessary to perform real estate transactions.

You can describe FHA amendment forms in detail, pointing out the difference between the FHA valuation and FHA commitment figures.

You can show him how to fill out a promissory note. I like to ask the homeowner what type of note he prefers: amortized, interest only, interest included, or straight. This usually serves to illustrate that he doesn't have the ability he once thought he had. Filling out a note properly can be very confusing. There are many things to remember.

If he still is not convinced, I will demonstrate how to fill out a deposit receipt for conventional and government-insured purchases. I will give him pointers to remember on GI purchases. If the home is in a price range above $50,000 so that government insured financing is not called for, I discuss the complicated details of conventional financing. I mention loan fees, escrow procedures, and the like.

Now you can see why I recommend a thorough knowledge of financing. To a homeowner, it is the most confusing part of any sale. By having a detailed knowledge of financing, we can use it better than anything else to re-seat the homeowner in his proper perspective, that of a listener rather than an advisor.

By bringing various real estate forms to Mr. Miller, the seller, you actually promote a listing. The forms are complicated. Homeowners need professional help. Fill out a few forms for the seller, add a fully rounded measure of financing detail, and you have concocted a recipe guaranteed to make the "do-it-himself" seller take another look at his real estate ability.

"You know, Mr. Miller, a home buyer can be fairly equated to a bride on her wedding day. Sometime during the day, before the ceremony, she takes a long, calculating look at her bridegroom and secretely wonders if she's doing the right thing. Of course the church has been reserved, all the guests are waiting, presents have been received. Fear of causing a scene has brought many a marriage to the altar that otherwise might not have occurred. Fortunately, most of these marriages turn out well.

"To the home buyer, everything is just beautiful on the day he signs a deposit receipt. However, during the waiting period, while the escrow procedures are being followed with ritual lack of speed, the buyer begins to think more prudently about his recent commitment. He continues shopping the home market.

"We know that homes are purchased on emotional reaction. The buyer's emotional level is at its highest point the day he signs a contract to purchase. From that moment, until he moves into his new house, his emotional interest wanes. A condition known as "buyer's jitters" occurs. If the purchase contract is not written properly, if every escrow detail has not been handled as it should, the chances are excellent that you will lose your buyer.

"If given an opportunity to make a choice whether or not to purchase, a buyer will invariably decide not to commit himself. This is logical. If he doesn't commit himself, he has not changed his status quo and hence, has nothing to fear.

"I am a professional, Mr. Miller. When I write a deposit receipt it is done properly, so that both buyer and seller are fully protected.

"Even with all our knowledge and ability, we lose some of our sales contracts because we can't hold the buyer to every contract he signs.

"Consider the position you're in. You don't have a fraction of the technical knowledge we do. Even if you got a buyer, it is extremely doubtful whether you would be able to hang on to him long enough to get an escrow closed.

"A moment ago, Mr. Miller, I asked you if you could sell me the house if I wanted to buy on a FHA basis. I mentioned FHA amendment forms. If they are not filled out properly and signed by both buyer and seller, the FHA will not process the papers and the escrow would never close.

"Different lenders have different point structures, Mr. Miller. I can bring you two sales contracts, one conventional and one government-insured, each bearing a different sales price, and the lower priced contract would actually net you more money. A knowledge of points would let you know which contract to accept. Are you familiar with institutional lender point structure quotations?

(Here you can use the "Story of Points" given in detail in Chapter 3.)

How is the home owner standing up under this barrage of information? Watch him closely. At any time he might turn to his wife and suggest that they go ahead and give you the listing. If so, you should fill out the contract without further comment, get it signed, and leave. Salesmen are all too prone to bask in the glory of their triumph after they get a signature. That is the time to go.

Remember I said that in our language, our listing conversation, we have to surprise our audience if we expect to keep their attention? Now's the time! You must be very careful when you use the next point. Let the homeowners see you are exaggerating intentionally—with humor.

In our example, the Millers are still not convinced. We continue.

"Do you have any children, Mr. Miller? Let me ask you this. If one of your boys suddenly complained of a severe stomach ache, would you lay him down on the kitchen table and begin carving on his stomach with a butcher knife to remove his appendix?

"A ridiculous question, isn't it? But that's actually what you're doing when you try to sell your home yourself. You are committing ECONOMIC QUACKERY! You are very probably going to butcher up the potential sale of your home simply because home selling is not your business.

"Medicine is not your business. The health of your family is the most important consideration in your life. When their health is at stake, you consult a man who is a specialist in health, a doctor.

"Mr. Miller, the most valuable material possession you have is your home. It is worth more money that any other object you own. You alone know all the things your home means to your wife, to your children, and to you.

"When you are faced with selling this valuable home, when you must commit yourself and your family to delivering clear title to your home dependent upon certain complicated terms and conditions of a contract, you need help from a person who is a specialist in home selling, a real estate salesman, Mr. Miller. I am that specialist!

"No matter how clever you might be with figures, how versed in salesmanship per se, you stand a very good chance of causing your entire family to suffer serious economic injury from your "do-it-yourself" kind of home selling.

"Real estate today is so complicated, so dynamic, requires such constant attention to detail, requires such a constant flow of education and re-education, that a person who does not spend every waking hour devoted to learning everything he can about it is left far behind when it comes to the ability to get the most out of a sales contract. Don't do this to your family, Mr. Miller."

Now be quiet. Let the husband and wife absorb the mass of information you have just dispensed. They will be thoroughly impressed, you can bank on that!

It is well to point out a few more truisms on the subject of FOR SALE BY OWNER selling before we consider the seller's confidence to be thoroughly swamped.

"Mr. Miller, I'd like to tell you one of the main reasons you will have so much trouble selling your home without my help.

"And you are not alone. Almost every other homeowner who tries to go it alone commits the same fundamental sales error. You over-sell your home to the prospective buyer.

"You're in an unenviable position. You only have this one house to sell. The buyer knows that. When a buyer is shown through a house by a real estate agent, that buyer knows that there are literally hundreds of homes that agent could have shown him, but he chose to show him your home. The buyer is half sold before he ever walks beyond the front door.

"When a buyer walks into your home, he expects to really get the 'treatment,' and he usually does. The housewife gushes at great length about the charms of her home, the neighbors, the schools. She expresses her distress at having to sell such a wonderful home, but after all, her husband was transferred, poor dear!

"The hard-working, hard-selling housewife is doing her best. But she isn't a trained salesman. She's never sold a pound of potatoes in her life before, and she's expected to sell a piece of property worth many thousands of dollars.

"She will go into great detail about the functionalism of the kitchen, the excellent condition of the furnace, the tasteful colors in the bedrooms, the new wallpaper in the guest bathroom. She will whirl about the yard as if she were modeling a new gown.

"She will be a vision of smiles, and radiance, and boorish high pressure salesmanship. She knows it. The buyer knows it. But the housewife doesn't think the buyer can tell. That's the pity of it all.

"Do you know who the most successful house salesmen are, Mrs. Miller? They are the salesmen who agree with the buyer. They are the salesmen who hardly speak when they are in a home with a buyer. They let the buyer go through by themselves.

"If the buyer says the ceiling is full of cracks, the successful salesman doesn't try to explain away the cracks. He agrees with the buyer. He says, 'Yes sir, that ceiling is sure a mess.'

"He keeps his mouth shut. He doesn't tell the buyer that this is the bathroom and this is the bedroom. The buyer knows that himself. A salesman can agree completely with the buyer as he runs the house to the ground and then do you know what happens?

"The buyer will say, 'You know, I think I can fix those cracks in the ceiling.'" And the salesman says, 'I think you can.' And the buyer says, 'I could repaint the bedrooms in an afternoon.' And the salesman agrees again. The buyer has to feel the salesman, or the homeowner, is on his side.

"And, Mrs. Miller, the buyer sells himself the house. This is accurate, Mrs. Miller. That's the way it really happens.

"But the housewife who is trying to sell her home without help is desperate. She quickly grows disgusted with the whole idea of selling. Every time the telephone rings or the doorbell buzzes, she prepares herself for another looker and another performance. 'Courage,' she tells herself, 'this might be the one.' She can't let him get away. So she musters up every last ounce of energy she has and begins bubbling with false enthusiasm all over again.

"And she can't do anything else! She doesn't have any other homes to sell.

"There's another bit of trouble you're going to have when you try to sell by yourselves. Whenever you leave your home, even if just for a half hour to shop at the corner grocery store, your house is off the market. Perhaps that's just the time a well-qualified buyer chooses to ring your doorbell. Chances are he won't come back. There are many other homes advertised for sale in the newspaper. He'll be looking at them by the time you return home.

"Buyers call on ads, and buyers look at homes, in order to eliminate them as possibilities. No matter what you may think, that is the sales psychology of the typical real estate buyer.

"It is always easier for them to eliminate a home as a possible new residence, and thereby remove the necessity of committing themselves, than it is for them to commit themselves.

"That's where the professional real estate salesman really earns his money. He is just that. A salesman! He knows when to speak. He knows when not to speak. He has all the answers about financing, schools, government regulations concerning purchase of a home, title and escrow procedures. He knows just how to get the buyer to want to commit himself. He knows just how to get you the money you want."

By now, the seller will have to admit, to himself at least, that he needs professional help.

Overcome Obstacle of Uncertainty

"When you let me go to work for you, here is exactly what you can expect. . . ."

At this point, you should outline in detail just how the home-owner's daily routine will be affected. A good lister should have this information on the tip of his tongue.

For example, "Next Tuesday morning we will have a sales meeting in our office, Mr. Miller, and after the meeting, I would like to bring the office staff through your home. We will be here about ten o'clock and will stay only a few minutes. We just want to see the floor plan and landscaping.

"I will send two appraisers to look at your home next week, but they will call for an appointment first. I will let you know what their appraisal is.

"Next week, when the multiple listing information cards are distributed to all the other cooperating offices, some salesmen from those offices will want to look at your home. They will call you for appointments. If someone calls for an appointment and it is not convenient to you, tell him so. I want to cause you the minimum of inconvenience. If there are certain hours of the day, or special days when you don't want to be disturbed, let me know."

This type of information helps to dispel fears. Now is the time, and only now, to "sell" your real estate firm.

(See THE LISTING MASTER - Gael Himmah Publishing Company - for more listing dialogues.)

Promote Your
Firm's Image

13

IT DOESN'T TAKE
long to sell the merits of your firm to the homeowner. You should

not spend more than five minutes on this topic. Sellers tire quickly.

Mention Your Professional Qualifications. You first mention any affiliations you have with local real estate boards, multiple listing services, state and national real estate boards. If you are Realtors, explain carefully just what that means. Explain how all members of your firm are sworn to uphold a very strict code of ethical conduct. Tell the homeowner how many salesmen your firm employs.

If you have a small firm with, say, three or less salesmen, you can stress the personalized attention your office gives every client. If you are associated with a larger firm with more than three salesmen, you can stress the sales volume of your organization.

Sometimes a seller will counter a lister from a large organization saying that when they list, they are going to sign with a small firm so they can get that personalized attention.

This is easy to answer effectively.

> Mr. Miller, people are the same whether they want to buy a pair of shoes or a new home. They want to go where they have a selection.
>
> It's well-established in the retail shoe sales industry, for example, that the best place to open a new shoe store is right next door to another shoe store. Both of the stores will profit because more people will shop for shoes on that block because the selection has doubled.
>
> Consider your own buying habits. If you wanted to buy a new suit, would you drive 2 miles in one direction where they had just 1 store, or would you drive 5 miles in another direction to a shopping area where there were 3 or 4 men's shops in a row?
>
> Of course you would drive to the area where the selection was the greatest. People who buy houses know this also. Transportation is no longer a problem. People will go to the location that will afford the greatest selection. They want the most for their time and money and they deserve to get it.
>
> That's what they find at our office. We have selection. We have made a substantial number of sales right in your neighborhood.

Give Homes Sold in the Client's Area. You should now go on with a short discussion of the specific homes you have sold in the immediate area. Name the names of the sellers if you can. It is interesting to the homeowners, and it lends authenticity to your whole discussion.

Tell of Your Firm's Characteristics. Discuss your firm's advertising policy. Explain a little about advertising for buyers. (This was discussed in Chapter 9.)

Tell something about the appearance of your office. I hope it is neat and clean. Many real estate offices look more like roadside fruit stands than business offices. If your office is located on a main street, all well and good. Point this out. But if it is located on a side street, you can explain this to your advantage.

Explain that people no longer drive down a street, suddenly see a large real estate sign and decide, on the spur of the moment, to buy a home. They don't veer off the road and pull up in front of the office with the impulse-buying gleam in their eyes like that of the female supermarket shopper.

Buying a home is serious business. Prospective buyers take a great deal of time, usually, in deciding just what real estate firm to contact. They will follow the newspaper advertisements, sometimes for days and days, before making a telephone call to the office.

They may drive around the city until they find a neighborhood they like. Then they will look for real estate signs displayed on the front lawns of different homes. They will arrive at a real estate office from the address given on the sign. The point being, if the real estate office has the merchandise to offer, and they market that merchandise properly, the buyer will find the office. It matters little where the office is located.

It's the story of the man with a monopoly. Everyone had to go to him. Every house is different. No matter how, or when, or for whom it was built, each house has a personality, an identity, all its own.

The real estate office that has a signed exclusive listing on a home has a monopoly on that one house. No one else can market it. A buyer who is interested in the house must come to him if he wants to buy it. If the buyer goes to a cooperating office, the listing agent will still enjoy a listing commission.

Discuss Inter-Office Cooperation. "Mr. Miller, the spirit of cooperation is so important to the healthy business climate we want to maintain in the real estate industry, that the multiple listing idea has caught on and become extremely successful all across the land.

"A real estate man is willing to share his monopoly with other real estate men. I welcome the opportunity. This is unheard of in other industries, Mr. Miller.

"A real estate man recognizes that his first duty is toward his client. His own interests are subordinate to this. By sharing his monopoly on a specific home, he is marketing the property for the homeowner in the most powerful fashion known to selling.

"Instead of just one office working to effect a sale, a virtual army of professional salesmen is working, at my direction, to bring you an acceptable sales contract.

"All this, Mr. Miller, my firm will do for you."

Write all the merits of your firm on a piece of paper. Memorize them. Be able to "rattle them off" when the opportunity arises.

Close Now—
Close Repeatedly

14

THE TIME HAS AR-
rived to "close" our prospect. You must get his signature on the list-

ing contract. He's convinced he needs professional help. He likes you as a professional sales person. He feels you represent a fine real estate office.

You've been rough on Mr. Miller. You've browbeaten him with information. You've re-shaped his thinking to a degree. You've made him feel unsure of himself in a real estate transaction. But he wants to continue to feel he is master of his household, so you had better change your tack!

Let Me Work for You

Be humble for a moment. It makes it easier for him to capitulate.

"Let me sell your home for you." Be sincere, genuine. Look directly at Mr. Miller when you talk to him.

"Let me go to work for you. I'll work very hard for you. I'll do a good job."

That's enough humility. You've made your point. The sellers want to be represented by a strong person.

I'll Get Loans. "Here's what I'll do for you, Mr. Miller. I'll get you three loan commitments so we'll know in advance just what kind of buyer we have to find. Until we do that, we're just guessing.

"I like to market a home just as if it were for sale in Macy's bargain basement! I want to have enough information about specific loans and interest rates, definitely committed from mortgage lenders, so that when a buyer asks, 'How much down, and how much a month,' I'll be able to tell him, 'If you put this much down, your payments will be this much a month; this much down and they'll be this much! You see, the buyer doesn't want to enter into a sales contract if the real estate agent isn't positive about the financing.

"If the real estate man says, 'I think we can get about this much at this rate of interest,' the buyer will never take out his check book.

"I want to show the buyer that I am a good salesman. Loan commitments are of primary importance. I'll get them for you, at no cost to you. I'll get a bank, a savings and loan, and an insurance company appraisal."

If the home is such that it might be sold under the terms of government-insured financing, be sure to explain this to the sellers. There is a charge for FHA and GI appraisals. The seller will have to pay $50 in advance for an FHA or GI appraisal.

It should be pointed out to the seller that there is a time lag between the time a government-insured appraisal is ordered and the time it is delivered. If the sellers are in a hurry for their money, they should order the appraisal at the time they sign the listing.

The successful lister will bring this up after he has the listing signed and deposited in his pocket. Don't confuse the sellers with a number of decisions.

I'll Give Information to the Top Salesmen. "In addition to getting you some loan commitments, I will pass out the information on your home to the top salesmen on our local real estate board.

"It's well known that 20% of the salesmen write 80% of the business. I know most of these salesmen personally. I will contact each of them with an enthusiastic report about your home."

I'll Keep Interest Alive. "In case your home doesn't sell very quickly, I'll keep putting out written notices, through our real estate board, concerning your home. This keeps interest alive among the salesmen."

At this time you should explain how the average home sells in 80 days after it goes on the market. (This was discussed in Chapter 3.)

We Will Produce Prospects. "We will run advertisements in the newspaper which will bring customers into our office who are interested in your type of home, Mr. Miller."

Be careful not to promise advertising on their home specifically. See Chapter 9 for a discussion of this.

I Will Qualify Buyers. "We will qualify buyers both financially and according to their desires, so that you experience the absolute minimum of inconvenience.

"We will always make a specific appointment with you to show the home. No more of those unexpected, and constant, interruptions."

I'll Get a Deposit. "Mr. Miller, if we show your home to a buyer who is interested in buying, we'll get a deposit. I'll write a sales contract that is binding upon him so that when I bring it to you for your approval, if you decide to accept it, the buyer will be bound. I insist on a deposit of at least $500 on a home such as yours.

"Mr. Miller, signing a contract with me merely gives me the privilege of bringing you offers. You can accept or reject those offers as you see fit. Whenever I bring you an offer, I will look it over to make certain it is a correctly drawn instrument, and then I will compute what you would net if you accepted it. If it is not enough, we will either counteroffer on your terms and conditions, or we will reject it completely.

You Are in Control. "You are in control completely. Your only obligation is that you have agreed to pay me my commission if I bring you an offer at full price on the terms you have prescribed.

"I'm sure you would be happy to pay me if I brought you an offer on your terms."

Write
the Contract

At this point, take out a listing contract and begin filling it in. Fill in the date of expiration at least four to six months hence. You don't have to explain this. In most cases the sellers won't even comment upon the termination date. But should they, explain that you expect their home to sell in a reasonable time, but the contract period should extend throughout the life of the sales escrow to protect your commission. The average home sells in 80 days. That's nearly three months. If the home is sold with government-insured financing, another three months could pass before the escrow closes. Hence, a six-month listing contract is necessary to protect the agent.

Enter
the Price

I have omitted the discussion of price from this chapter because we discussed it in detail in Chapter 4. I find that unless the seller brings it up earlier in the conversation, the decision as to price can be arrived at while you are filling in the listing contract.

When it is practically ready for signature, ask the sellers what price you should specify. If price has been discussed earlier, fill it in without comment. If it is brought up now for the first time, your explanation of pricing will prove to be an excellent break in the intensity of the moment.

By allowing you to discuss price at this time, the sellers are acknowledging that they will sign the listing contract.

Get the
Contract Signed

I do not believe in the petty, non-professional sales method of dropping your pen, or rolling it across the table toward the customer so that he has to grab it to keep it from falling, as a means of getting the pen in his hand.

When the contract is filled out, stand up, walk to where the seller is sitting, and hand your pen to him. After he takes the pen, hand him the contract and point with your finger to the line where you want him to write his name.

"Please sign here, Mr. Miller."

Congratulations! You've just taken a good listing. A little more effort, and you'll be putting money in the bank.

(See THE LISTING MASTER – Gael Himmah Publishing Company – for additional "closing" diaglogues.)

Answering a
Seller's Objections

15

WHEN YOU ARE IN A
seller's living room working for a listing, discussing the pros and cons

of selling with professional help; when you are thus on your own, here is when your own level of professionalism will be demonstrated. Here is where you have to think "on your feet." Here is where dollars are made and lost. Be alert!

Every homeowner has a few pet objections that he will cast before the listing agent. He full well expects these objections to confound the real estate salesman so that he will leave a chastened man, and the seller will thereafter be able to chart his own course in his own time.

There are only a limited number of objections possible. There are excellent answers for each of them. This is true because there is a real need for professional real estate services. The ability of the lister to successfully answer any and all objections is dependent upon his ability to prove the true worth of his services. They are one and the same.

In this chapter, I will list, and answer, the most common objections. Extractions from the answers can be used to successfully answer practically any problem that arises during the course of securing a listing.

Let's assume that just as we are filling out a listing form, Mr. Miller pops up with one or more of these objections.

A Friend
in the Business

I have a friend in the Real Estate business. If I list, I will have to list with him.

Answer. "I know just how you feel, Mr. Miller. You feel like you're really on the spot if you sign a contract with anyone other than your friend.

"But think of your home a moment. This house represents the most valuable piece of real property you own. When you market it to the public, you are competing with a great many other people.

"Every one of those people wants to realize the maximum number of dollars from the sale of his home. Most of these other homeowners have employed professional real estate help. You're going to have to have the most highly skilled real estate help you can get.

"Consider, for example, that one of your children needed a dangerous, highly specialized, operation. Would you feel obligated to go down the street to the family doctor and ask him to perform the operation? Of course not! You wouldn't even think of the family doctor for such an operation. You would want to get the best surgeon in the country. The health of your child is so important to you that you would do whatever was necessary to provide the finest for your family.

"Your home is the most valuable material possession of your entire family. Don't feel obligated to put its sale into the hands of someone merely because he is a friend.

"You want the best. You deserve the best. Your family is depending upon your judgment, and your decision. You know they'll stand beside you. Give them the best real estate assistance available.

"If your friend happens to be the most highly skilled real estate salesman in the area, by all means commit your home, your hard earned equity, to his keeping.

"Ask yourself, 'Is he the best for me?'

"You know, Mr. Miller, I have often thought how difficult it must be for a stock broker, when one of his close friends comes to him and asks him for investment advice.

"As sure as anything, the stock will probably begin to drop in value as soon as the friend makes the purchase. I know how I would feel if I were the broker. I would feel I had let my friend down. And I would probably resent him just a little for putting me on the spot.

"We all know the old adage about not doing business with friends. That's a time-proven way of ending a friendship instantly!

"By contacting your friend and asking him to market your home for you, you are putting him in a delicate position. If he doesn't get you the absolute top dollar for your home, he will feel that he has failed you. He will wonder what you think of him.

"Many times there will be little things about the décor of the home that, if corrected, would help in the sale. I have known many salesmen in the position of your friend who just can't bring themselves to make the suggestions. This, alone, can cost you hundreds of dollars.

"Years ago, in San Francisco, a friend of mine called to advise me he wanted me to sell his home. I listed it, but I wasn't happy.

"His house was a mess, but being such good friends, I couldn't bring myself to suggest that he clean up the house. It took a long time to sell the home because of its condition. My friend was not happy with the slow sale, but he didn't feel he could give me a push, if I needed one. He had actually forced me to perform as a non-professional.

"You certainly want the most dollars from your home, Mr. Miller. Is your friendship so close that you would sacrifice dollars for it? Actually, your friend may be much happier if you contract with some other agent. He will be able to sell it as a cooperating salesman, and you have not forced him into the position of being your employee.

"Looking at it from your position, Mr. Miller, there are times during the course of selling a home, that the homeowner might want to lay it on the line with the listing agent. If that agent was your close friend, you would just have to grin and bear it.

"No matter how you look at it, listing with a friend almost always costs the seller money.

"The real estate industry is about the same as other businesses in several respects. In real estate, about 80% of the property is sold by 20% of the salesmen. Is your friend one of these top producers? Can you be certain that he is?

"If your friend is such a capable sales person, why do you suppose he is not here at this time? No doubt he feels he would be putting you on the spot if he asked for the contract on your home.

"That's what I mean by the awkward situations that will arise should you seriously consider him as your agent. First you're on the spot, then he's on the spot. Your friendly relationship will never be the same.

"I'm a good real estate salesman, Mr. Miller. I love my profession. I'm proud of my job. You can count on me to do a good job for you. I'll get you the most dollars for your home.

"If you still want to sign with your friend, I will put his name on the bottom of the contract when I finish filling it out. Whose name shall I put on it?"

I have never had a seller tell me to put any name other than my own on the listing form after going through this presentation.

You Can Sell
My Home Anyway

I'm going to have to list my home with Uncle Joe, but you can still sell it.

Answer. "It's not as easy as that for me, Mr. Miller. When I sell my own listing, I make 20% more money than if I sell a home listed through a cooperating office.

"Taxes take more than 25% of every dollar I make as it is. You are suggesting that I toss another 20% down the drain! I'm too good a salesman for that. I work too hard to be expected to give so much away.

"Even if your home is on multiple listing, the listing agent is the most important motivating force in selling.

"Unless Uncle Joe is a cracker jack salesman, you had better seriously reconsider your decision. All salesmen will work hardest on properties contracted through their own office simply because they make more money by doing so. Commit the sale of your home to the real estate office that has the most impressive sales record. Let me tell you about my office. . . ."

I Don't Want to
Tie Up My Home

I don't want to tie my home up for 90 days.

Answer. "Mr. Miller, I don't make a dime unless I bring you an acceptable sales contract on your home. When you hire me to find you a buyer, you've actually tied me up for the term of the contract.

"By definition, a listing is a unilateral contract. It's one-sided. You have given me your pledge to pay me a commission only if I sell your home at the price and terms you select. You're in control. I'm working for you. You have put the burden of performance upon my shoulders, which is exactly where it should be. This is my business."

I Don't Like MLS

I don't like multiple listing service.

Answer. For goodness sake, don't argue with the seller. This is not the time to debate the merits of multiple listings.

"Multiple listing has definite advantages, Mr. Miller, but many people prefer to market their homes without the hustle and bustle sometimes associated with the sale of homes through multiple listing.

"The exposure of the home to sales people is necessarily limited, but we, in my office, have been very successful in selling homes without the help of cooperating brokerage offices."

Let's Wait Until Spring

I want to wait until spring. That's when homes sell best.

Answer. "That seems logical, I know, but actually homes sell all year long. Homes sell even on Christmas Day, if you can imagine that!

"Many other homeowners feel the same as you, that spring is the best time to sell. But that's when you run into all the competition.

"Comes spring, and more homes come on the market than any other time of year. Many sales are made, but also, more for sale property remains unsold. You are competing with many more homeowners for the home buyers' dollars. Don't look for competition. Put your home on the market now, when it is more conspicuous."

I Want To Find
a New Home First

I don't want to list until I find a home I want to buy.

Answer. "You might be making a serious error, Mr. Miller. Let's assume that you spend a great deal of time looking at homes and finally you find that dream house. When you make an offer, you will find that you are in a terrible bargaining position because you will be a 'contingent' buyer. Your offer will be contingent upon the sale of your present home.

"The owner of the home you want to buy isn't going to stand for that. He will insist on a 'release' clause in the sales contract. His home will stay on the market and if he gets an offer he likes better than yours, you will have to come up with the money required to complete your purchase or void the contract.

"You can't afford to make payments on two homes at the same time so your entire family is disappointed when you lose the home you searched for so long.

"Even worse, if you were to receive a low offer on your present home while you had it on the market, trying to finalize your purchase, you would likely be so anxious to have the new house that you would accept.

"You have thus put yourself in the position of paying top dollar for the house you are buying, and accepting rock bottom price for the house you are selling.

"By signing with me now, you are reversing your position. When you get an offer, you can determine the closing and occupancy periods yourself. When you find your dream house, you are in an excellent bargaining position, because your home is sold and in escrow.

"Hence, you have not put yourself under pressure. You have waited to get top dollar for the home you are selling and you can make a real "buy" on your new home. Think about it. You will see I am right. Place your home for sale now and put yourself in a good bargaining position!"

Securing Exclusive
Agency Listings

16

THE   EXCLUSIVE
agency listing is the greatest boon to money making since the oil

well! As defined in Chapter 6, an exclusive agency listing is a listing contract given by a homeowner to a real estate salesman wherein the salesman's office has the exclusive right to market the property to the exclusion of all other real estate agents, but the homeowner retains the right to sell the property himself to a buyer he finds himself. If the homeowner can find such a buyer, he does not pay the real estate agent any commission monies.

Certainly the most desirable kind of listing contract, from the real estater's point of view, is an unconditional exclusive listing contract. This type of listing should be the primary goal of all listers. However, circumstances are such that it is often not practical for a homeowner to commit himself to the strict provisions of an unconditional exclusive listing.

It would be unwise for the professional lister to refuse to accept any type of listing other than an unconditional exclusive until the seller sees things his way. By then, another alert real estate salesman would have the property tied up on an exclusive agency basis.

Again, let me remind you never to lose sight of the fact that your primary goal as an income-producing lister is to eliminate your competition. This is where the exclusive agency listing is most valuable.

Prospective Buyer. I have often called on a FOR SALE BY OWNER and had him tell me that he would like to list but he has an interested buyer who will give his decision in a few days.

The prospective buyer probably won't return, but I can't blame the homeowner for waiting to see. He has devoted time, energy, and money trying to find a buyer himself. Once he feels he is close to victory, it is extremely difficult to secure a listing. An exclusive agency listing is the answer.

Prepaid Ad. For another example, consider that when you, the lister, call on the homeowner who is displaying a FOR SALE BY OWNER sign on his front lawn, the seller seems receptive to all your sales suggestions and recommendations. You feel that a listing is close at hand.

But the homeowner tells you he is running an advertisement in the local newspaper and he had to pay for the ad in advance. He doesn't think it would be very wise to sign an unconditional exclusive listing with you and just throw all that advertising money away. He's got a point there!

You explain how futile it is for him to depend upon newspaper advertisements to sell his home. You advise him that it takes an average of 250 telephone calls into a real estate office before the person calling buys the home advertised. Realizing that these figures are the product of professional skills, you tell the homeowner that at that rate, it would take him several years of constant advertising to sell his home. The cost of all those newspaper ads would far exceed the real estate commission.

You also explain to this homeowner that people call on real estate advertisements to eliminate the home rather than to find the home. This serves to magnify the owner's sales problems.

You have exhausted every alternative suggestion. You have tried, with no success, to explain why the homeowner should sign with you that moment, advertising money or no advertising money. The very fact that he has been spending his hard-earned money on newspaper ads, you explain to him, should be reason enough for him to employ professional help. He must have a real need to sell or else he wouldn't be advertising.

All this falls on deaf ears. Don't give up the ship! Bring out that cunning money magnet, the exclusive agency listing. We want to get him to sign something. That's one of the cardinal secrets of sales success. No matter what, get the customer to sign something. Start a sale if you can't complete one!

Don't continue to debate the homeowner on the prudence of doing his own advertising. You can see he isn't about to be talked into anything. So agree with him!

"Mr. Jones," you explain, "I don't blame you for wanting to wait until your advertisement runs out before you sign a contract with me. You just might find a buyer.

"Incidentally, should you find a buyer, or at least get hold of someone who seems genuinely interested in purchasing your home, feel free to call on me at any time for assistance. You can tell the buyer I'm a friend of the family if you want to. I'd be happy to write up the sales contract for you and qualify the buyer with no charge or obligation to you. It's my way of thanking you for your courtesy to me today."

This throws the homeowner off balance, and fills him with a reciprocal sense of obligation. One just naturally feels obligated to return a favor when it was tendered spontaneously at a time of need.

"Mr. Jones, I have a suggestion that I think you'll like. My office uses a contract called an exclusive agency. It is not the kind of contract you are familiar with. It gives me the privilege of bringing you offers on your home, but it does not prevent you from continuing to try to sell your home yourself. It's as if we were in competition with each other, each trying as hard as we could to produce an acceptable sales contract on your home before the other.

"You do not lose any of the sales privileges you enjoy right now. The difference is that while you are trying to affect a sale by yourself, you are also employing an office staffed with full time, professional real estate salesmen. Each of these salesmen is an expert in his own right in producing sales on homes. These people will work for you every day of the week, all day long. You don't pay them a dime.

"Your only obligation to us is that you will pay us a commission if we produce a sale on your home at a price, and with terms, that are completely acceptable to you. You remain firmly in control of the sale of your home. We are working for you. Then, when you have decided to throw in the sponge on your do-it-yourself sales efforts and elect to bow out of the picture, the contract will become a regular unconditional type exclusive.

"The advantage of the future automatic conversion is that until your contract becomes unconditional, my real estate board will not accept it for the multiple listing service. You do get a much greater exposure to real estate sales people when your property is marketed through a multiple listing service. When you get tired of trying to sell by yourself, your property will automatically have the benefits of the multiple exposure to the market.

"While your home is on an exclusive agency basis, you are still enjoying the services of my entire office."

You must be careful, at this juncture, to assay the seller's degree of understanding of the mechanics of the exclusive agency listing. Most sellers do not clearly understand the first time they hear it. If you sense that the homeowner is in a bit of a quandry, repeat what you've just said. Take your time. You'll get the listing. That's for sure!

"Mr. Jones," you continue, "when you give me an exclusive agency on your home, you get an added benefit. My office has a policy that if, during the term of an exclusive agency, the seller should sell his home himself, my office, at the seller's request, will handle all of the escrow work, take care of the financing, and process the entire transaction, all at no expense to the seller."

Fortunately, this doesn't happen very often.

"You look skeptical, Mr. Jones. Actually, it is very seldom that a homeowner ever beats us to a sale. Perhaps once or twice a year. But when that does happen, the seller has been so thrilled at the service we gave him that he spread the word about our office to his friends and neighbors and we profit, there's no doubt about that.

"So you see, when you give me an exclusive agency, you not only have a full-time staff of professionals helping you, but in the event you make a sale yourself, you have eliminated one of the greatest obstacles the independent seller can have, lack of knowledge. You have all the facilities of my firm right behind you, ready and willing to give you all the help you need."

By a simple development of this theme, you will have no trouble at all in securing a listing. A seller would have to have a personality defect not to accept this proposal. He has everything to gain and absolutely nothing to lose. And the lister has a new listing!

Filling Out
the Listing

Use the regular exclusive listing form you always use. Insert the following legend in the body of the listing, following the description of the property:

AUTHORIZATION TO SELL

Lafayette ...., California, ... October 11, 19......

In consideration of the services of .... BONANZA REALTY, INC. ....,
hereinafter called the agent, I hereby list with said agent, exclusively and irrevocably, for a period of time beginning
...... October 11 ......, 19......, and ending ...... June 30 ......, 19......, and grant said agent the
exclusive and irrevocable right to sell within said time for...... Thirty Seven Thousand and no/100----
($37,000.00----) Dollars, and to accept a deposit thereon, the following described property in the
...... Area of Lafayette ...... County of ...... Contra Costa ....State of California, to-wit:

Lot and improvements commonly known as 2252 Little Lane.

The purchase price shall be payable as follows: All cash to seller.

This is an EXCLUSIVE AGENCY listing from date until October 21, 19 ,

during which term seller is not obligated to the commission statement

for buyers he should secure through his own efforts.

Property may be placed on Multiple Listing Service at agent's option.

I hereby agree to pay the agent as commission ....SIX..(6).... ....per cent of the selling price herein named, whether said property is sold by said agent, or by me, or by another agent, or through some other source, or if said property is transferred, conveyed, leased or withdrawn from sale during the time set forth herein.

If within ten days after the termination of this listing, said agent notifies me in writing personally, or by mail, that during its life, he negotiated with persons named by him, and sale is made within one hundred eighty(180) days after the termination of this contract to any person so named, I agree to pay the agent the commission provided for herein.

If a deposit is forfeited, one-half thereof shall go to said agent as commission and one-half to me, provided, however the agent's share shall not exceed the amount of the above named commission.

Evidence of title to be in the form of a Policy of Title Insurance issued by ....any......... TITLE COMPANY and paid for by the buyer.

Thirty days allowed for examination of title, following receipt of the deposit. Taxes (July 1 basis), interest, insurance, loan trust funds (if indebtedness is being assumed) and rents to be prorated. Insurance may be cancelled. When sold as herein provided, I will convey said property to the buyer by a grant deed, and when notified of sale I will immediately upon request deposit with said Title Company for delivery, said deed and any other documents and instructions necessary to complete the transaction. If objection to title is reported, I agree to take immediate steps to clear title and buyer shall within five days after title is reported cleared by the Title Company, deposit the full purchase price in escrow.

Notice of sale hereunder may be given to me by telephone, orally, or by mail to the address given below, or by personal service.

Time is of the essence hereof. In the event of the failure of a buyer to perform any of the terms hereof, all rights of such buyer shall immediately cease and terminate.

We hereby acknowledge receipt of a copy of this contract.

Address ....2252 Little Lane.......................

.....Lafayette...California...............................

Telephone ....284-9776.................................

In consideration of the above listing, the undersigned agent agrees to use diligence in procuring a buyer.

Lloyd L. Vickey

Deborah M. Vickey
Seller.

BONANZA REALTY, INC.

By _Jack Hannah_
Real Estate Agent.

Figure 8

This is an exclusive agency listing from date until _____,
during which term seller is not obligated to the commission statement for buyers he should secure through his own efforts.

The overall term of the listing should be filled out just as you would a regular unconditional exclusive, for five or six months. Then, in the exclusive agency amendment, you insert the term of the exclusive agency.

For instance, let's presume the homeowner wanted to run his newspaper advertisement another ten days. We would then fill in the exclusive agency amendment clause showing the termination date of the exclusive agency to be ten days from the commencement date of the listing. After that date, the listing would automatically become a regular unconditional exclusive. It is not necessary to make another trip to the seller's home to get another listing contract signed. One listing does the job of two.

If the listing is to be submitted to multiple listing service, include on the listing form the statement: "Property may be placed on multiple listing service at agent's option." (See Figure 8.)

It is apparent just how the use of the exclusive agency listing develops into an unconditional exclusive and a multiple listing. It relieves some of the sales pressure from the homeowner while he is getting to know you.

If the seller wants to try a little longer himself, use the exclusive agency listing. If the seller isn't quite sure he wants to "tie up his home" with a real estate firm, use the exclusive agency listing. If the seller wants to give newspaper advertising a whirl, use the exclusive agency listing. If the seller wants to wait and see if his buying prospect returns, use the exclusive agency listing.

Above all, if you can't sign the seller to an unconditional exclusive listing, use the exclusive agency listing. But first try, and try again, to secure an unconditional exculsive. The exclusive agency is always an alternative.

Filling Out
a Listing Card

17

ONCE THE LISTING IS
taken, you must merchandise and market it properly or else you

won't realize any money from your efforts nor rewards for your time.

Filling out the informational listing card which will be sent to all the salesmen working on the property (I shall presume this is done through a multiple listing service) is of vital importance.

Certainly all the pertinent information about the house must be given. The information on the loan commitments should be included. These are things any salesman can do. But there are three areas that bear special attention.

Give
Directions

Somewhere on the card there should be a space wherein the listing agent can give directions to the property. Listing the nearest cross street is a great help. Inserting the unfamiliar name of subdivision areas, such as Wildwood Manor Number Two, is of little help to the salesman trying to find the street.

The names of subdivisions that are easily identified by everyone are excellent aids, but the lister must be wary. Unless he is certain the subdivision name is really easily recognized, use the cross street. You want to make money, not teach a course on subdivision geography!

Occupancy
Section

The next section on the listing that bears special consideration is the one dealing with occupancy dates.

Many real estate people automatically insert "Upon Recordation Of Deed," or "Upon Close Of Escrow" in this section. It should be pointed out to the seller that the implications of occupancy are manifold.

If it is possbile, because of the nature of the sales contract, for a sudden, unexpected closing to occur, the seller should be so advised in advance. We can't expect a seller to move overnight.

You should advise the seller not to commit himself to give

occupancy until a few days after close of escrow or, better still, "By Agreement."

This way, "By Agreement," the seller will consider every offer on his property in its proper light. If the offer was high enough, I'm sure the seller could be out by midnight. I know I would be if I got enough money for my home. Occupancy dates are worth money to the seller. We must represent the seller just as fairly as we can. Hence, we must advise him of the mechanics of occupancy.

Many times, a low offer requesting immediate occupancy can be successfully countered, the seller allowing immediate occupancy for a higher price.

If the seller had agreed to give immediate occupancy in the first place, he would have lost this bargaining tool when it came time to sign a sales contract.

Occupancy by agreement should be recommended to all sellers unless the seller is able to vacate on very short notice and isn't interested in the bargaining aspect of the occupancy clause.

Remarks
Section

The final, and by far the most important, section of the information listing card is the space that allows for comments by the listing agent.

The information card is actually the first advertisement on the property. The home is advertised, by means of the card, to all of the sales people who will add the home to their inventory of saleable property.

Consider the average multiple listing service. Scores of new listings are published each week in the form of informational cards. When our card is published, it will be sandwiched among a large stack of cards.

All of the cards are trying to attract the attention of the busy real estate salesmen. A salesman can only look at five or ten new listings from each publication. That makes the odds against our new listing being inspected by all salesmen very great.

What we have to do is sound so enthusiastic or interesting in the remarks we have put on the card that the other salesmen will say, "Maybe he's got something here. I'd better take a look."

One of my salesmen listed a modern, three-bedroom, two-bath ranch home situated in a large subdivision. There were many similar homes for sale in the immediate area. None of the homes were receiving attention from real estate salesmen. It looked bleak, but my salesman used his imagination.

He utilized the power of the listing information card to overcome this lack of salesman interest. Recognizing he had to get the other salesmen to inspect his listing before they could sell it, confident that once they saw it they would appreciate its excellent condition and tasteful, Far Eastern décor, he decided to tease their curiosity.

On the listing card he described the home as an ORIENTAL RANCHER. Of course there is no such animal in captivity as an Oriental rancher, but real estate salesmen are always looking for something different to show their customers.

The telephones in our office practically leaped off their cradles as soon as the listing was distributed through our multiple listing service. All the salesmen who called had the same question, "What is an Oriental rancher?"

And our reply was always the same. "Take a look at the house. You'll have to see for yourself."

They drove to the home, inspected it, and found it to be a rather ordinary ranch style home with some Oriental decoration. But they included the property in their stock of merchandise. Within the month, one of them sold the home. The carefully planned use of the listing information card was directly responsible for putting money in my salesman's pocket.

In another instance, we referred to a home as a CAPE RANCHER. The result was identical.

Another time one of my salesmen noted in the "remarks" section of the listing information card that his new listing had an old-fashioned, stone water well with bucket and all.

Bucket serviced water wells are rare in the San Francisco Bay

Area. Troops of salesmen arrived at the home just to see the wishing well. In the course of their well inspection, usually as an afterthought, they decided to look through the house. Again, the same result. The home sold soon thereafter.

We have to give as much information as space permits, yet we can't abbreviate. Abbreviations indicate an absence of quality. They give evidence of sloppiness.

Use words that are "punchy." Be careful not to use words that have a dreamy, calm, sleepy quality. We want the sales people to get excited about our new listing. We don't want to lull them to sleep.

Positively the worst word you can use is "charm." It's a wonderful word when talking to buyers, but you can never hope to stimulate real estate salesmen to the point of charging out to see a new listing if you described the home as "charming." This is the most "unpunchy" word in our language.

The word "nice" is about as ineffectual. We've got to put zip in our message. Words like "terrific" and "wonderful" are badly overworked. The more unusual the word, the more eye-catching. Since your card space is limited, choose your words carefully.

> Custom rock fireplace!—extreme seclusion!—trees!—unusual, gigantia, a zingo rancher!—freeform patio, pine sweet, plenty big rooms!—price massacred!—yeowee, here's utopia!—Wow, what a view!—$4,000 underpriced!—desperate seller!—hurry!

Here are all examples of words with punch, words with "let's take a look" appeal.

When I see a description saying, for example, covered patio, I wonder what it's covered with. Could be dirt, could be leaves, could be a louvered shelter. Be explicit, be careful with language, but be exciting!

How to
Service Listings

18

sional lister has taken the listing, his work is far from done. Remember, you have promised to secure several loan commitments on the home. You must contact the different institutional lenders you had in mind and make arrangements for each of them to inspect the house. You must prepare the listing information card carefully, as I have explained in Chapter 17.

Consider just how the typical homeowner feels after he has signed a listing contract. No matter how carefully the listing agent has explained the sequence of events that are to soon occur, the homeowner will still prepare himself, and his household, for an onslaught of real estate salesmen and their customers that he is certain will soon befall him.

As already noted, one of the reasons a homeowner resists listing with a real estate salesman is the owner's fear of the unknown qualities of selling through an agent. He has visions of hordes of real estate agents and their customers pouring through his home hour after hour.

After the seller has braced himself, after he has expended the energy required to steel his mind to the distasteful prospect of living in a fishbowl, and the invasion of the real estate people does not occur, he is more deeply baffled than ever.

He begins the tortuous task of soul searching, or more accurately, house searching. He thinks something is wrong with his home. He needs reassurance and counseling. That's what the considerate lister can belay by keeping in close, and constant, contact with the seller.

Phone Sellers
Weekly

After a listing is taken you should telephone the seller at least once each week. When I take a new listing, I make notes on my desk calendar to call the sellers every week for the entire term of the listing. I can't afford to leave this to memory.

I can thus report the reactions of the other salesmen in my office to the homeowner and I can, at the same time, ask how many showings the home has had from other cooperating real estate firms.

You should give the sellers information and instruction on what to do while their home is being shown. They should be advised, in a gracious manner, not to enter into the conversation between the buyer and the agent unless asked by the agent. Three's a crowd!

The seller should be given tips on how to spruce up his house for inspection. The National Association of Real Estate Boards has some excellent pamphlets designed especially for this function. When we receive a new listing in my office, we immediately send the homeowners a pamphlet containing friendly tips on how to show their home to its best advantage. We accompany this pamphlet with a "form" note on letterhead paper thanking the sellers for their listing and suggesting they might find the enclosed pamphlet helpful.

You can pass along to the homeowner information about new listings of comparable homes in the area of the seller's home. Information about general sales activity is always appreciated by the seller.

No matter what is discussed, the homeowner will feel reassured just hearing from you often, on a regular basis.

Many questions arise in the minds of sellers during the term their homes are offered for sale. A word or two from a patient, understanding real estate salesman is usually enough to assuage these thorns of concern. As each of these problem questions is answered, the seller will become increasingly grateful for his decision to seek professional help.

Get the Price
Reduced

After a property has been on the market a few weeks, you will invariably have a more accurate idea as to the probable sales price of the home than you had at the time of listing, for the other salesmen in your office and salesmen from cooperating offices, will all have expressed their opinions.

I recommend to sellers that they collect the business cards of real estate salesmen from other cooperative offices who inspect the home.

Thank you for the opportunity

to manage the sale of your home.

Others have found the enclosed

booklet helpful in preparing their

home to show off at its best. We

are sending you this copy in the

spirit of friendly suggestion,

which will help us -- to help you --

obtain the best price for your

home in the shortest possible time.

BONANZA REALTY, INC.

Figure 9

After a week or so, collect these cards, phone each of the sales-men, and ask for their opinion as to price. It is surprising, but most homes sell within $1,000, plus or minus, of the average price quoted by a group of cooperating salesmen.

This average price information should be relayed immediately to the seller. Then I ask the seller what he is going to do about adjusting his price. After all, he set the price himself! This method of pricing puts the "shoe on the other foot" and it is highly professional. The seller, thus, will not be calling me complaining about a lack of sales activity.

You should feel it your moral duty to give all your current information, your conclusions about the probable sales price, to the homeowners. Whether they adjust their price to the new figure is their decision.

If the number of prospective buyer showings of the new listing is meager, you must determine the cause of resistance and overcome it. You won't make any money if you don't!

Once again, let me point out the three factors that affect the sale of a home: condition, location, and price.

Obviously location is something that cannot be remedied. If the problem rests with condition or price, you must tell the sellers immediately and recommend steps that should be taken to correct the problem.

Some salesmen make a separate file on each of their listings and keep an accurate record of every owner-contact made, salesmen remarks and suggestions, appraisal opinions, everything that affected the listing. A note on a scrap of paper is sufficient, but be sure to date each entry.

After a period of time, the file should have many notations. Such a detailed chronicle of facts is very persuasive when shown to a homeowner who doesn't want to adjust his price to a realistic figure.

Write
a Letter

During the term of a listing, if the sales activity has been slow, write a letter to the homeowners outlining the reason for the slow sale. If you feel the price needs adjusting, say it. A letter will give you the opportunity of expressing yourself in a professional manner. You can plan your remarks in advance! Here is an example of such a letter:

Mr. and Mrs. Henry Carstairs
15 Holly Hill Road
Alamo, California

Dear Mr. and Mrs. Carstairs,

I am concerned that we have not yet produced an acceptable sales
contract on your home. A home such as yours should sell within 80
or 90 days, and we have been working on the property nearly four
months.

As we have discussed on many occasions, I believe your price is the
problem.

The location and condition are excellent. There is an abundance of
mortgage loan money available at attractive interest rates. The
market for single family dwellings has been active. In fact, we have
sold over 40 homes within the last four weeks.

Prospective buyers who inspect your home feel they can buy more
house than yours for the same price you are asking.

Salesmen from cooperating real estate offices have expressed similar
opinions. I believe we set the price too high originally. The sales
resistance we have experienced on your property supports this
opinion.

Let's try reducing the price $1,500. I'll stop by Saturday morning to
discuss this with you.

With kindest regards, I am

> Very truly yours,
> BONANZA REALTY, INC.
>
> Gael C. Himmah
> Broker

Get the Listing
Renewed

If a listing term is about to expire, you should make a trip to
the sellers' home with a fresh listing form in your pocket. Make sure
both the sellers are home, just as you did when you first took the
listing. You're going to be under a figurative magnifying glass again,
so be prepared.

If you have maintained a file on the listing, and I do recommend
it, take it with you. Tell the seller you want to renew the listing
on his home. Don't be evasive. Come right out with it.

Describe, in as much detail as possible, everything you have done to market his property. Tell him once again of the appraisal opinions of the cooperating real estate salesmen. If his price is too high, tell him so. Advise him of any unusual market conditions.

Inform him of the current status of mortgage loan financing. You must have an opinion of why his home has not sold. Be frank with the homeowner. He will respect you for it. And then take out your listing contract, just as before, hand it to him, and show him where to sign his name.

Giving the seller attention, keeping in constant communication, in all, servicing the listing after it is taken will earn you a nice listing commission plus the additional bonus of knowing you have given professional service to those who depended upon you.

Develop a
Daily Schedule

19

LISTING IS NOT A
profession that can be successfully practiced in a haphazard fashion.

To be successful, the listing agent must schedule his time, allocate his activities, continually assess his results.

As in all phases of the real estate industry, there are so many avenues of potential revenue accrual that it is a simple matter to become mesmerized by the glitter of fool's gold beckoning at the end of each of the many rainbows.

To become a jack-of-all-trades and the master of none is a horrendous mistake. Pick a specific field within an industry, and then specialize within that field. And then specialize within your specialty.

Listing is a specialty of the general brokerage real estate industry. Single family dwellings are a special facet within the phylum of listing in general. There are many methods of pursuing listings of single family dwellings. Specialize in these. Choose only a few methods and develop your prowess in them to such a plane that you are head and shoulders above your competition.

Everyone will soon adapt himself, by measure of his inherent talents and abilities, to the specific types of listing activity he wishes to follow.

I am going to suggest a schedule for listing that was extremely successful for me and has proven its merit to scores of successful listers I have helped in my specialty.

Phone Expired Listings. Each morning, when you first arrive at the office, telephone all of the multiple listings whose terms have expired the required length of time. Regardless of whether there is only one such listing or if there are 50, phone them all.

Don't try to get too selective. Listings on dirty homes earn commissions. Listings on "overpriced" homes earn commissions. Listings on homes in areas that are not as desirable as others earn money. Every home will sell! There is a buyer for every home.

Low priced listings sell more rapidly than high priced listings as a rule. This is because the buying market for the lower priced homes is greater in number. This does not mean that you should slight the expensive homes. If you get the listing, and if that home was ever meant to sell, you're going to get some money out of it.

If you dial a number and the telephone has been disconnected, get in touch with the neighbors. Usually they can give you a forwarding address so you can get in touch with the homeowner.

Cold Canvass Phone Calls. I recommend making five cold canvass telephone calls daily. I have found the best time for these calls is after one o'clock in the afternoon. This will vary from area to area. If a salesman has a problem forming good work habits, he might do better to make these calls first thing in the morning. He will know that each day, as soon as he enters his office, he will pick up his telephone and go to work.

The reason I choose the afternoon for cold canvass calls is that the housewife is normally most busy with housework in the morning. The children have come home from school for lunch and are, by one o'clock, back in school. The housewife has time to think of something other than her house duties for a moment. A call from a gracious real estate salesman soliciting her help is almost a welcome break in the day's routine.

House Calls. You should make at least three FOR SALE BY OWNER calls daily, in person. The best time for these calls is right after the telephone canvass calls, in the afternoon. If you wait until school is out, the housewife will again be too busy to give you much attention.

Check Newspaper Ads. Finally, you should, each day, clip from the newspapers all of the FOR SALE BY OWNER advertisements. Paste each one on a blank, lined card and use the card to record the history of your contacts with the owners.

This is important. You will soon have many listing leads. These notes will become invaluable. You will never remember what you said to whom on what date, and what they said to you!

Follow up each listing contact. If they don't list the first time, heaven forbid, they will list the next. I recommend a personal call to each seller who has an advertisement in the newspaper. He's ready to sign a listing contract; he's spending his money on advertising. It won't take him long to grow tired of this folly and let a real estate firm spend their money instead. A personal call is always more fruitful than a telephone contact.

If a real estate salesman followed faithfully the schedule for listing I have herein outlined, his days would be so filled with activity that he would have little time for selling. It certainly isn't a complicated schedule. It doesn't have to be.

The professional listing agent, working full time at listing, should secure 15 to 30 new listings each month. If you will follow this schedule, your days will soon be so busy that you will have a hard time finding a spare moment to get to the bank to deposit your commission checks. When you list, you are forced to sell. When you list on a scheduled format, you are forced to make a great deal of money!

(See REAL ESTATE SELLING MAGIC – Gael Himmah Publishing Company – for salesman schedule forms.)

Profit

Producing Letters

20

TWO OF THE MOST powerful tools a listing specialist can use are *letters* and *flowers*.

When pursuing a listing, I never forget my competition. I know I'm not the only real estate agent the homeowner is speaking to. I want to create a memorable impression. I want the homeowner to remember me. I must present myself in a manner that is different than my competition. I want to do something special.

Flowers are the means! Coupled with a well-composed listing letter, flowers are a master stroke of salesmanship.

I believe every salesman should locate a florist shop where he can buy a dozen carnations at a reasonable price. Incidentally, I don't favor roses because they don't last very long. Carnations are rugged, sweet-smelling, and pretty! That's a tough combination to beat.

Let me give you an example of this letter-flower team in action.

Listing
Incentive Plan

In my office, I am anxious to maintain a good supply of listings, and I recognize a certain listing inertia is present in most real estate salesmen.

It seems as soon as a new salesman has his first blaze of glory and has developed substantial accounts receivable, his sales aggressiveness begins to taper off. This is the classic pattern of most salesmen in every industry.

Eventually, the real estate salesman recognizes that he can earn an adequate income by selling a few homes each month and securing listings as the opportunity arises. Although he has learned the technique of listing, human nature decrees that he should not expend so much effort on listing activities as he had in the past.

His income suffers, but it's the course of least resistance. Only the rare salesman continues listing aggressively. He is amassing a tremendous income, but he is the exception. I recognize this condition as being true, and have created an incentive program that is very effective.

When a new salesman comes to work in my office, he is assigned to one of the other salesmen who has learned the listing technique and demonstrated success in listing. It is the responsibility of the experienced salesman to help the new man in listing. He will show the new man how to develop leads, how to follow the leads, and he will actually go with him and write up one or two listing contracts for him. I call these "dual listings."

A listing thus taken will be the sole property of the new man. This is important because the new man, realizing that all the listing commission will be his own, will be more eager to learn how to merchandise his listing.

When a listing is brought into the office in this manner, I pay the experienced salesman $50. He is paid immediately upon receipt of the listing. I don't care if the listing sells or not. That is of secondary importance. The new man rapidly learns how to list. He is gaining confidence by having listings on the books.

The experienced man has an opportunity to earn some easy money. But more important, by taking the new man out in the field, he is regaining his taste for listing. He gets the feel of it again. There is no teacher as thorough as teaching! By teaching the new man, the experienced man is learning. The new man is constantly prodding the experienced man, suggesting they go after another listing, and vice versa.

I have two rules in this dual listing incentive program. I will pay an experienced man only for the first five listings he gets a new man. By then, the new man will not require any more help and will be on his own.

Also, the listings must be "saleable." I define a saleable listing as being for a minimum term of 90 days, located within our marketing area, of the exclusive right to sell or exclusive agency type, and priced "somewhere within reason." My pricing policy precludes me from being more specific. I retain the right of being the sole judge of what is, and what is not, saleable. I only turn down about two listings a year as being unsaleable. My salesmen know that if the price is reasonable, nothing will be excluded.

I was going to give an example of the letter-flower combination in action.

Late one Saturday afternoon, two of my salesmen came into my office with a problem. They were a dual listing team and had just returned from a home which they were trying to list.

When they had arrived at the home, they were greeted by the housewife. She told them that her husband had been transferred to Oregon and had already reported for work in Portland. He only returned home on weekends and was at that moment taking a shower. She said that several other real estate salesmen had shown an interest in listing their home.

She invited my two salesmen to return to her home at six o'clock that evening when her husband would meet with all the salesmen from the different offices, listen to their stories, and then give his listing to one of them.

My salesmen had thanked her and returned to the office to see me. They asked if they should return at six o'clock as the housewife had suggested. They wanted advice.

The answer was easy. I explained that they should not go back to the house when all the other real estate salesmen would be there. That would be a free-for-all. My salesmen would have to do something to pique the husband's curiosity, something that would cause him to delay his decision for a day. They were unable to speak to him directly.

A listing letter would be the perfect messenger. I suggested that they write the following letter to the husband.

Mr. Willard Smithen
1015 Mayhew Lane
Pleasant Hill, California

Dear Mr. Smithen,

I will not have an opportunity to meet you this evening at six o'clock, although I am very interested in securing a listing on your home.

We have an exceptional sales-to-listings ratio in my office, due in great measure to our extraordinary marketing procedures. I know you can appreciate that I do not want my competitors to learn of these in detail.

I am certain you would be interested in learning more about my office. Unless I hear from you to the contrary, I will stop by your home tomorrow morning at eleven o'clock.

Please convey my thanks to Mrs. Smithen for her courtesy this afternoon.

> Very truly yours,
> BONANZA REALTY, INC.
>
> Philip D. Randle
> Salesman

I also suggested that my salesmen buy a bouquet of carnations for Mrs. Smithen.

The new salesman signed his name to the letter, bought the flowers, and returned to the Smithen home about five-thirty, only half an hour before all the other salesmen were due to arrive. He gave the letter to Mrs. Smithen, asking her to deliver it to her husband, and he presented her with the flowers, thanking her personally for her graciousness earlier in the day.

Mrs. Smithen was thrilled. She said she hadn't received flowers since her wedding day. She promised to give the letter to her husband.

My salesman left. There was nothing more to do but wait until 11 o'clock the next day. But he was in for a surprise. At ten o'clock the next morning, Mr. and Mrs. Smithen arrived at our office. They announced they wanted to list their home with us. They didn't even ask about our "extraordinary" marketing procedures.

Mrs. Smithen whispered to my salesman that after receiving the flowers, she wouldn't let her husband give the listing to anyone else, even if he had wanted to.

I think all those other competitive real estate salesmen who were at the Smithen home that Saturday evening are still wondering what they did wrong. They didn't do anything wrong. We just did things right!

A letter and flowers—don't overlook their value.

The subject of writing letters to homeowners as a tool for securing listings is a constant topic of conversation in my office. I believe letters are one of the finest devices a professional lister can employ. Consider that practically no salesman takes the time, or makes the effort, to write to his listing prospects.

Many times, after the lister has made the acquaintance of the housewife, he doesn't follow up properly. Perhaps he thinks she will remember him. She will, if no other salesman bothers to ring her doorbell. But if this is the case, the listing is probably not too desirable anyway.

Better than leaving the memory of the housewife to chance and supposition, write her a letter. Thank her for her courtesy. Flatter her on the condition of her home. Give her information about your firm. Use your office's letterhead stationery.

Many is the time I have returned to a home after meeting the wife, and found my listing letter lying on the table in the living room beside all business cards of real estate salesmen. It doesn't take much imagination to guess what caught the husband's eye when he came home from work and glanced at that table.

Many times we have thought of a perfect reply to some remark made in an earlier conversation. Usually the opportunity to use the reply never again presents itself. But a letter will serve us perfectly. When you are back in your office after an unsuccessful listing conversation with a homeowner, you have time to think of what went wrong. When you have made your decision and found a solution, a listing letter is the ideal medium for transmitting the information to the homeowner.

A letter leaves a good impression. It gives the addressee an opportunity to study your suggestions and recommendations. It gives him a chance to appraise the sender's business acumen.

In an earlier chapter we learned the Ten Magic Questions. Let's suppose, for example, that the housewife we were speaking to told us her husband travels in his job and would not be home for three or four days. We should send her a listing letter immediately. We don't want to lose the rapport we've achieved. And her husband will enjoy reading it when he returns. It is a nice introduction for you.

Following are samples of listing letters. They are self explanatory. Similar letters can be used in your personal listing program.

These are letters that have proven their effectiveness. They have led directly to listings in my firm.

Standard
Listing Letter

Here is a letter I sent when my office was a small, recently formed sales office. It was addressed to a prospective seller whom I had contacted through a cold canvass telephone call.

It is a simple matter to amend this letter so it can be used as a standard, office listing letter. It has a certain appeal that resulted in a listing when my office was new.

Mr. Edwin F. Jacobs
3376 South Walker Avenue
Moraga, California

Dear Mr. Jacobs,

Pursuant to our telephone conversation this evening, I am writing this brief letter to acquaint you with my firm.

Although recently formed, we have a sales staff composed of experienced real estate salesmen who are thoroughly familiar with Moraga properties.

Being young as a firm, we don't have scores of other listings. This means your property will receive the maximum attention from our sales staff.

You can see our style of advertising in the Oakland Tribune and the Contra Costa Times. It is effective advertising.

We have to sell properties. We need the money! Given the opportunity, we'll do a fine job for you.

I will stop by in the near future and discuss our services in more detail.

Please accept my thanks for your courtesy during our telephone conversation.

With kindest regards, I am

Very truly yours,
BONANZA REALTY, INC.

Gael C. Himmah
Broker

The Exclusive
Agency Letter

One afternoon I spotted a FOR SALE BY OWNER sign in front of a lovely, ranch-style home. I rang the doorbell and proceeded to ask the lady who answered the Ten Magic Questions.

I learned that her husband, an engineer, had been transferred to Los Angeles and was anxious to sell his home, but he disliked real estate salesmen with a passion, and insisted his wife sell the home herself. He had already reported for work in Los Angeles and was home only on weekends.

His wife, let's call her Mrs. Baylor, had an FHA appraisal on her home and had shown the property to many people, but she had not yet received any offers. She had not tried advertising in the newspapers. She wanted to give the property to a real estate agent but her husband would not agree.

I asked her if her husband might be influenced by receiving a well-composed letter outlining some of the points we had been discussing. She thought that was an excellent idea.

I wrote a letter on the exclusive agency theme because I didn't want Mr. Baylor to think I was usurping all his rights of "do-it-himselfism." I wanted to take it easy in my approach.

When you write a listing letter, remember to be direct in your statements. Don't be subtle, and don't be evasive.

Mr. Robert Baylor
20 Russell Avenue
Lafayette, California

Dear Mr. Baylor,

I am writing this letter soliciting a listing on your home. This afternoon your wife was so kind as to give me 15 or 20 minutes to explain something about my firm and the sale of your home in particular. I am writing this letter in response to her suggestion. I fully understand how irritating it is to be pestered continually by real estate salesmen trying to list your home.

I am certain Mrs. Baylor will discuss the suggestions I made today. However, I would like to outline in detail a proposal of mine which she felt would interest you.

It is axiomatic in the real estate business that very few professional real estate salesmen will ever show a home to a prospective purchaser unless that home is listed with some broker. A listing is the only protection the salesman has and, of course, all of us in this business live on commissions.

I don't blame you one bit for trying to sell your home yourself. I'd probably consider doing the same if I were you.

However, there are reasons too numerous to mention here explaining why a purchaser seldom buys direct from an owner. But still there is that slim chance that you might sell direct to a buyer.

Due to the exceptional sales-to-listings ratio our sales staff enjoys, Bonanza Realty Inc. offers an unusual type of listing arrangement to a seller who still wants to try to sell his home himself. This is known as an EXCLUSIVE AGENCY listing.

There is a statement on the listing form which reads, "Sellers are not obligated to the commission statement for purchasers they should secure through their own efforts."

That is self-explanatory. You do not lose any of your privileges as a seller under the terms of this listing. If you sell your home to one of your buyers, at any price you desire, you pay us no commission at all. You can advertise and do anything you are doing right now to promote the sale of your home.

Bonanza Realty, Inc., would be competing with you, in a sense, to bring you an acceptable sales contract before you can secure one yourself. Of course, we would net you at least as much money as you would net if you sold the home yourself. Buyers are willing to pay at least 6% more for the security of buying through a licensed real estate firm.

Under the terms of such a listing you are, in fact, hiring an entire staff of full-time professional salesmen to work for you at no expense to you.

In addition, should you find a buyer during the term of this exclusive agency listing, at your request, we would be happy to act as your personal real estate broker—write the appropriate sales contracts, qualify the buyers, place the loan, handle all the escrow work, etc., all at NO EXPENSE TO YOU!

We do this because an owner very seldom beats us in our "race" to bring in an acceptable offer first. Also, the few times we have lost the "race," the sellers were so pleased with the calibre of the work we did for them in completing their sales, that they most kindly recommended several other persons to us whose homes we listed and sold.

Considering the loan information Mrs. Baylor gave me, I believe we can net you approximately $3,000 at a sales price of $21,500.

I would appreciate an opportunity to meet with you personally and discuss the sale of your home in more detail.

Mrs. Baylor, please accept my thanks for your courtesy and graciousness this afternoon.

With kindest regards, I am

> Very truly yours,
> BONANZA REALTY, INC.
>
> Gael C. Himmah
> Broker

This letter was actually sent to a seller under the conditions described. The husband was so interested in the information given about his chances of selling his home himself that he signed an unconditional multiple listing contract. Their home sold in 82 days.

Salesmen from at least 20 different offices had been soliciting this listing. Mr. Baylor told me that the receipt of my listing letter had helped to convince him that he should list with Bonanza.

A Flattering Letter

I discovered a beautiful home offered FOR SALE BY OWNER. I rang the doorbell and found the owner to be the proverbial "little old lady." She was very cordial and invited me to inspect her home. It was decorated in excellent taste, and neat as a pin. The yard was landscaped so that it looked like a magazine cover photo.

This lady, Mrs. Dixon, had a love affair with her house. She did all the gardening herself and she had the home custom-built to her own specifications. She confessed that the only reason she didn't give her property to a realtor was because she felt they would not feel as "close" to her home as she thought necessary. She wanted the realtor to love her home as she did.

I returned to my office and wrote her the following letter, using descriptive phrases that she had used herself. I had been careful to make note of the way she described her home to me.

Mrs. Ruth B. Dixon
92 Gary Street
Walnut Creek, California

Dear Mrs. Dixon,

I have just returned to the office after my visit to your charming home. I want to thank you for being so gracious. It was very considerate of you to invite me in.

I was so impressed with the appearance of your home that I was moved to write this short letter. The beautiful setting, the quiet country lane, the flowering trees and cool green lawns make your home a veritable paradise.

The exterior elevation of your home is particularly appealing. The rustic front makes it appear to be solid and well-built. It blends very well with your landscaping. I can see many hours of hard work that you must have spent on landscaping and maintenance.

The interior has a feeling of spaciousness, due, I am certain, to the exceptionally well-conceived floor plan and the light, bright rooms. Those large windows surely make a difference! There is a picture view from each one.

The balance of this letter was a basic listing letter describing the number of salesmen in my office, etc.

Mrs. Dixon was so thrilled when she received my letter that she phoned me immediately.

"Mr. Himmah," she enthused over the telephone, "I loved your letter. Why, you feel the same way I do about my house. I'm glad I found you. You can sell my house for me and I won't have to worry anymore."

That letter put nearly $800 in my pocket.

A Timid Seller

I know of a short street bordered with cozy homes. Homes are seldom for sale along this street but if a salesman can get a listing here, it's money in the bank!

I drive down this street every so often, looking for signs, and on this particular day I was in luck. A large, hand-lettered FOR

SALE BY OWNER sign was nailed to a stake in the front lawn of a house.

I stopped my car, walked to the front door, and rang the doorbell. There was no answer although I could hear footsteps inside. I returned to my office and called the telephone number shown on the sign. Again, no answer.

I drove back to the home and checked with a neighbor who explained that the young housewife was extremely shy, had a chronically ill child, and never answered her doorbell, and since her husband put up the sign, she wouldn't even answer the phone.

They had to sell. He had a new job in the North, but he worked seven days a week, was never home, and didn't have the time or inclination to talk to real estate salesmen. A letter to him was the only answer.

Mr. M. W. Rath
1202 Vacation Place
Orinda, California

Dear Mr. Rath,

I stopped by your home today hoping to meet you, but unfortunately I missed you.

I spoke to John Williams, your neighbor, and he mentioned that your wife was concerned over having salesmen disturbing the baby in the morning should you decide to list your property.

I know just how she feels since I have a small child of my own. In fact, my wife assures me that there is nothing more trying for a wife than to attempt to maintain a home in a semblance of order and have scores of real estate salesmen troop through the house.

Should you be kind enough to give my office the opportunity to sell your home, I would be happy to note on the listing card that the home is to be shown in the afternoon only. Also, we could list any other requirements you might have. If a salesman calls for an appointment to show your home and it is not convenient, feel free to tell him so.

I intend to do everything I possibly can to make the sale of your home as pleasant as possible and I shall be most happy to work out any details that could cause you concern. In my office, above all else, we respect the privacy of sellers.

Please contact me at your earliest convenience as I am very anxious to get to work for you.

With kindest regards, I am

Very truly yours,
BONANZA REALTY, INC.

Gael C. Himmah
Broker

Mr. Rath telephoned me several days later and I listed his home. It sold within the week. A listing letter was the only way of getting in touch with this homeowner, and it performed masterfully.

The Appraisal Letter

A letter was sent to a homeowner who was interested in getting a price recommendation before signing a listing contract. This seller would not tell me what price he had in mind. His house was a custom-built contemporary in an exclusive neighborhood.

Mr. James Appleton
1812 Poplar Street
Lafayette, California

Dear Mr. Appleton,

Thank you for the opportunity of inspecting your property. Your home, and the grounds, are certainly in excellent condition. They will "show" very nicely to prospective buyers. This always means a good deal toward a speedy sale at the top market dollar.

Constructing the figure from a careful analysis of the physical inspection of your property and the information from our Residential Cost Appraisal Handbook, I find that the replacement value of your property is approximately $42,500. This figure is based upon allowances made for depreciation and obsolescence which are inherent factors in the appraisal structure of any property.

With this figure as a starting point, I then had to consider the supply and demand for similar homes in the area in which your property is located, and the season of the year with respect to the popularity of swimming pool properties as we approach the hot summer months.

Weighing all factors, I have arrived at a fair market value of somewhere between $43,000 and $44,000.

My recommendation is to offer your property for sale at $43,750.

We at Bonanza Realty, Inc. will be pleased to represent you in the sale of your home. I will stop by to see you in a few days.

With kindest regards, I am

> Very truly yours,
> BONANZA REALTY, INC.
>
> Gael C. Himmah
> Broker

Mr. Appleton was impressed with the straightforward approach of my letter. I returned to his home several days later and left with the listing. A price appraisal had been the obstacle here. The letter gave me the boost I needed.

Letter to a Building Contractor

Here is a letter I sent to a building contractor who had a new home under construction in my marketing area. I have sent similar letters to many building contractors with excellent results. It has to be "newsy" and give the contractor several alternatives. I always include a listing contract which requires only the contractor's signature. They are busy and appreciate this time-saving gesture.

Mr. Bud Harper
Bud Harper Construction Company
1441 Franklin Street
Danville, California

Dear Mr. Harper,

I have been following with great interest the progress of construction of the home you are building on Michael Street in Danville.

I would like to secure a listing on this home. Due to the apparent nearness of completion, the time is right to expose this fine home to a volume of potential buyers.

The members of my office, and I, have been answering a steady flow of inquiries on this property. We have been giving out information at a prodigious rate.

The majority of real estate sales people in this area just won't work on a property unless it is listed with some local broker. If we had one of our signs on your home, I know the volume of cooperating Realtor calls into our office requesting information would be considerable.

Certainly I would prefer an exclusive right to sell-type listing, either an office exclusive or a multiple listing service exclusive, but I'll take anything I can get!

To promote sales response from the other 900 or so cooperating salesmen who are members of our real estate board, I will prepare, and send out, detailed information sheets on the house to all offices who are active in this area and price range.

I am extremely pleased with the sales potential of the home. Considering the location, floor plan, quality, footage and price, I feel certain we can bring you an acceptable sales contract.

All of the salesmen in my office would certainly appreciate the opportunity of working for you.

I am enclosing an exclusive listing contract filled out as well as I could without conferring with you personally. Should there be any entries which do not meet with your approval, please cross them out, insert the correct information, initial the changes and sign the listing. Please keep one copy for your records and mail the original to me in the self-addressed envelope I have enclosed with this letter.

I shall be anxiously awaiting your reply.

With kindest regards, I am

> Very truly yours,
> BONANZA REALTY, INC.
>
> Gael C. Himmah
> Broker

Consider how many more listings you would have if you mailed just one listing letter a day. It doesn't take much time to write a letter. The dividends will be fantastic!

Effective

Newspaper Advertising

21

SOME EXCELLENT
books have been written on this subject. I want to add a few com-

ments to what has already been committed to paper. For a real estate office forming its advertising policy, there are some basic considerations which I believe to be extremely important.

There are rule-of-thumb dollar amounts that can be applied toward establishing a ratio between salesmen in the office and advertising dollars for the office budget. I believe a minimum budget of at least $50 per man per month should be allocated for newspaper advertising. This will vary from one part of the country to another.

Providing extra advertising dollars for the top income producers in the office, and identifying the specific salesmen by name in the ads, is a well-considered incentive method of advertising. This directs the greatest number of buying prospects to the best salesmen, the salesmen who do the most to earn dollars for the Company.

The Right
Newspaper

When faced with the problem of choosing between several different newspapers, I recommend that the classified sections of all the newspapers in question be spread out on a table, side by side.

Some newspapers have a better "look" than others. The print is darker and easier to read. The columns are more evenly spaced. There is not too much heavy black type which tends to obscure the copy.

Which newspapers appear to receive the most real estate advertising? This is significant, but it does not necessarily mean that they are the papers to use to the exclusion of the others. I discovered one local paper that was hardly used at all by the other Realtors in my marketing area. We enjoyed unbelievably good results from our advertising dollars spent in that paper. We basked in the sunlight of a virtual monopoly on the use of the classified pages of that paper for nearly a year, until the other Realtors began to catch on. You should look for such a paper. They do exist. Experiment!

When you have selected several papers that have the circulation in the areas you want to cover, when you have selected the papers that are easy on the eyes, then read the real estate advertisements appearing in them. Read them carefully!

Run a tape on your adding machine and determine the average price of the homes offered for sale in each of the papers.

I believe in standing out like a sore thumb when it comes to advertising. If the average listing price is $20,000 for example, you should try homes priced above or below this figure.

I found a newspaper in my area that seemed to be used almost exclusively for the advertisement of lower priced homes. With some experimentation to learn the style of copy that attracted readership, we found this newspaper to bring in the best results on very high priced homes. We are still using this same paper today for the advertisement of our expensive properties and most of the other real estate firms are still limiting their use of it to low priced homes.

If the temper of advertising is sedate, or downright stuffy, give the readers something to talk about! Use imagination in advertising. Don't forget humor. Be newsy in your copy. Sound excited.

Think before you write!

Ads
with Punch

Here are some examples of newspaper ads used in my office that initiated excellent buyer response.

Gold, Gold

The Bonanza Boys strike it rich! You claim jumpers check this for sure. Brand new classic colonial Moraga mansion. Nearly 1700 feet of living area in this four-bedroom, two-bath chateau. The rooms are huge—huge—WOWEE—gigantic! Formal dining room, family room, 21-foot living room with massive custom fireplace. Tile entry. Built-in vanities in full-tiled baths. Walk-in closets. One bedroom 11 x 20 and it's not even the Master! An authentic Southern

Colonial set on a big corner lot. Terrific view. Construction is starting so check this today. Just $2,800 down to a new FHA. Only $141 per month. Full price—$26,300.
BONANZA REALTY, INC.
Lafayette
Call 284-1122—ANYTIME

Cannibal Casserole

Price chewed to the bone! A once-in-a-lifetime buy. Custom four-bedroom, two-bath rancher. Complete redwood exterior. Massive beamed ceilings in living room. Custom fireplace. Commanding view of entire Lafayette Valley. Scores of mature trees. Lovely gardens accentuate the plush setting. Exclusive neighborhood. SECLUDED. Spic 'n span. Here's a bargain! Owner antsy. Hurry. Only $19,950.
BONANZA REALTY, INC.

Chicken Fat and Turnips

A friendly rancher for that family that wants a truly cheerful setting. Seclusion supreme! Hidden away on a cozy court. Immaculate custom rancher. Three gigantic bedrooms, separate 20-foot family room, electric kitchen, custom fireplace, wall-to-wall carpets and drapes. Flagstone patio with massive brick bar-b-que, doll house, cabana. Oodles of giant shade trees. Gorgeous landscaping. Sacrifice. Hurry. $27,950.
BONANZA REALTY, INC.

Here are some sample headings that were very successful in gaining readership:

Rudabaga

Ain't a'growin' here, jest happy kids. . . .

Skunked in
Burton Valley

Firm sale fell through. . . .

Aardvark

Outstanding. . . .

Sweet 'n Piney

Like a high Sierra mountain estate. Alpine air scented with pine. . . .

Pop Sugar

recommends this zingo rancher. . . .

Fancy Dan

Here's a buy. . . .

Yewoee

The buy of the year! . . .

Sweet Cider

Summer's outstanding bargain. . . .

Gold Bug

gonna bite when you inspect this truly immaculate, architect designed, four-bedroom, two-bath, Lafayette farm house. . . .

Auction Sale

of sorts. Name your own price and terms. . . .

Massacre

FLASH! Quality builder must sell for peanuts. Give 'im a scalpin'. . . .

Tickled Pink

You'll love it too. . . .

Hawaii Free

round trip for two (includes hotel) awarded when you purchase this secluded, five-bedroom, three and a half-bath home. . . .

Tightwads

Here's your chance. . . .

Pixie Gold

Just listed! . . .

Texas Ten

It's big, wranglers! . . .

Solitude

John Muir's beloved valley—The Alhambra—offers beauty and calm unequaled. Now you can own a prestige home in the "rich man's" paradise. . . .

Seven Fat Rats

ain't 'nuff to buy this secluded rancher. Transferred sellers need SOME money!

Tabasco Hot

Happy Valley Brittany rancher. . . .

Ghastly

neighbors? Tiny house? Want privacy? . . .

Yo Yo Jo

our chief appraiser, recommends. . . .

Les Vents D'Avignon

Picturesque as the Parisian countryside. . . .

Possum Pie

'n cracklins, hog shank 'n grits! Nothin's sweeter than this Cane Sugar Lafayette rancher. . . .

Sail Away to Valhalla

but don't leave Lafayette! . . .

You can see the headings are punchy. They catch your eye. The sentences in the ads must be short, descriptive, but not too flowery. You can save a good deal of money by omitting the "adjectives that point out" from the copy—*a, an, the, this, that, these, those.*

You must convey urgency in your ads. "Unusual circumstances force immediate sale . . ." is overworked but still effective. Variations of this phrase will reward the copywriter with an imagination.

Words in the body of the ad—seclusion, trees, immaculate,

custom fireplace, views, spacious, paint and save—all highlight points of buyer motivation. Use them.

Listing in volume is such a refined art that it is nothing short of tragic when the advertising created to support the lister's efforts does not produce buyers for the types of properties listed. Advertise with deep thought and freshly stirred imagination. Advertise to alert your real estate competitors. If you can interest them, the buyers will call!

(See THE LISTING MASTER – Gael Himmah Publishing Company – for a study of key words which make newspaper advertising much more effective.)

Negotiating the
Listing Contract

22

AS THE PERFECT
conclusion to our listing adventure, the procedure of getting an offer

accepted is most fitting. All the listings in the world aren't of any value to you unless they are sold.

When you are notified that there is a sales contract in existence on one of your listings, you should immediately contact your sellers and make an appointment to present the contract to them. It is preferable that the sellers meet in your office. There is always an advantage to conducting business in one's own office. However, if that should prove inconvenient to the sellers, a meeting in their home will be fine.

If any of the conditions of the contract are unusual, it would be well to go over the specific terms and conditions of the offer with the selling salesman before it is presented to the homeowners.

I never insist upon knowing the price, terms or conditions of an offer before presenting it. Your position is that of the representative of the sellers who will answer questions put to him by the sellers. You will interpret the contract for the sellers. You are not there to pass judgment on an offer unless your advice is solicited.

If the selling salesman wants to discuss the specifics of his contract with me, I am happy to comply.

For the purpose of this discussion, let's assume that we have an offer on the Miller home written by a salesman from a cooperating office. You have made an appointment to present the offer at the seller's home.

Don't divulge any information about the offer over the telephone. If asked for such information by the seller, advise him that you do not have the offer in front of you and that there are so many specific points to consider that you would be doing him an injustice to try to explain anything before studying the contract.

As soon as you and the selling salesman arrive at the seller's home, be sure to introduce the selling salesman to the sellers. It is a mistake to immediately launch into a dissection of the offer. Talk about anything but business for a short time.

Can you remember some time in your childhood when you were promised a weekend camping trip with your Dad? For days you conjured thoughts of cooking your dinner on a campfire. You thrilled to the thought of sleeping under the stars in your new sleeping bag.

The magic of anticipation somehow made the well-charred dinner, which Dad had dropped several times into the ashes, taste like a gourmet's masterpiece. The night under the stars, when the temperature dropped to 39 degrees and coyotes howled menacingly all night so that you didn't sleep a wink, seemed the most relaxing period of rest you ever had.

Don't, by any means, overlook the power of anticipation. Until the seller has seen the contract, he can pretend the offer is anything he wants. He is king for just a bit, so don't spoil it.

He will already be making plans to move his furniture into the new home. He will be selling himself on the idea of accepting the offer.

This period of conversation also gives the selling salesman the opportunity of getting better acquainted. This is important. Soon he will have the responsibility of presenting the buyer's case. After several minutes of friendly banter, ask the selling salesman if you can see the contract. It should always be carried by the selling salesman. This is the time to explain to the sellers the precise mechanics of the moment, the procedure of hearing an offer, the function of the real estate agents.

Explain
Your Function

"Mr. Miller," you begin, after you have the contract in your hand, but before you have begun to read it, "I'd like to explain just what my function is tonight.

"I represent you and Mrs. Miller. I am your agent. Mr. Bronson, the salesman here, represents the buyers. I will examine the sales contract to make certain it is a legal, properly prepared document should its terms meet with your approval.

"I will explain any conditions that are confusing. Should you have any questions whatsoever about the contract, I will answer them for you.

"I am working for you. Now, if you will give me just a minute, I will read the contract and then give it to you."

The anticipation remains just a little longer.

This explanation is necessary for the sellers' information. They don't know just what to expect. They have probably heard tales about real estate agents pressuring any offer they get on the home-owners just to make a fast dollar.

With two agents with them in the same room, they have a propensity to feel challenged. To combat this, they adopt a defensive attitude. We must prevent this before it develops.

As soon as you have finished reading the contract, making certain all is in order, hand a copy to Mr. Miller and another copy to Mrs. Miller.

Let them read it without comment from you. I have seen sellers look over a sales contract for a moment and ask, "Where do I sign?" If that happened very often, this chapter wouldn't be necessary!

When they are through reading the contract, outline its conditions for them. Usually, the first comment from the seller will be an exclamation about the price. (We will assume this offer is low.) Don't be concerned.

Interpret Contract
for Sellers

"Mr. Miller," you reply, "have you read all of the contract?"

Remember, when you ask a question, you are in command of the conversation. When you call a person by name, you short circuit his mind for a split second. That's long enough.

"Do you understand all the terms and conditions?"

Mr. Miller will still be objecting about the price. "Because of the technicalities of mortgage loan financing, Mr. Miller, due in part to the complicated GI and FHA procedures, a homeowner can accept one offer at a lower sales price than another offer and still walk away from the title company with more money than if he had accepted the higher sales price.

"Considering the tax and insurance prorations, the escrow costs and other fees associated with selling a home, the only thing you should be interested in is the amount of money you're going to have when you leave your home for the last time. Give me just a minute and I'll work it out for you. I'll just be a moment."

The selling salesman, to this point, has not spoken a word about the contract. For the moment, you want to direct the conversation. You can't let Mr. Miller get too upset over the offered price. If this happens, his pride will soon take charge and he will not be able to back down later in the evening and accept the lower price even if he wants to.

As soon as you have computed, as nearly as possible, just how much the seller will net if he accepts the contract as it is written, and be conservative with the seller's money, ask him a few more questions. Don't offer the amount yet.

Seller Gives
Minimum Figure

"Mr. Miller, forgetting real estate commissions and the existing mortgage loan on your home, how much money would you take right now, in cash, to give me the key to your home and walk away from it? Assume your furniture and your moving plans were all taken care of. Don't be greedy, now. Be realistic. I feel you know as much about the sales prices of homes like this as I do."

Let's assume, for this example, that you have computed Mr. Miller's net to be $7,700. We have to throw him off balance a little.

"Would you accept $6,500?"

"Of course not. You think I'm crazy?"

You try again, always suggesting. Don't make him think too deeply. "Would you take $7,000?"

Mr. Miller counters. "When I listed my house with you I told you I wanted $8,500." He doesn't sound quite so angry.

"I know you did, Mr. Miller. And don't think I wouldn't like to sell your home at the full listed price. I'd make more money for myself if I did. But at least we have someone who thinks enough of your home to give us a nice deposit. We should at least see what we can do with it.

"Would you take $8,000, Mr. Miller?" You see a spark in his eyes.

"I might take $8,000, but those other figures are just plain nuts. I wasn't planning on coming down $500."

Now you give him the net figure on his home as the offer is written. "If you were to accept this contract tonight, Mr. Miller, you would walk away from the title company with $7,700 in your pocket."

Don't try to defend this figure. You haven't tried to talk him into anything. You have just been asking him questions. It is important to get the seller talking about net amounts instead of sales price. This figure of $7,700 is just too much for our seller to bear.

"I told you $8,000, not $7,700. I won't take a penny less!"

Now you've got to make a decision. You've got a deal, and you know it, but should you work on the seller to bring him down the additional $300? Perhaps you should counter offer back and try to get the buyers up the $300.

Maybe it would be best to split the difference and have each of the parties absorb $150. Under no circumstances should a real estate agent ever cut a commission. But we want to have a finalized contract tonight. A counter offer is out.

"Mr. Miller, we are only $300 apart. Should you refuse this contract, expecting to receive an additional $300 from the sale of your home, you are, in effect, gambling $28,500, the offering price, in hopes of making $300.

"You would never make that kind of a bet in Las Vegas. You might risk $300 trying to win $28,500, but to risk $28,500 to try to make $300 makes it a horrible business decision. I know you'll agree with that."

Explain the dangers of changing a single word of the sales contract.

"Please understand, Mr. Miller, I don't want to influence your decision other than to explain the mechanics of the sale. You don't have to accept this contract. Of course it took two months to get this one, but the decision is yours."

Overcome
Objections

"We always sleep on it," Mr. Miller explains.

"What do you mean by that, Mr. Miller?"

"Whenever we have an important decision, Mrs. Miller and I always wait a day before we make up our minds."

"I see you have a new car in the driveway, Mr. Miller. How long did it take you and your wife to decide you would like to buy it after you first saw it?"

"We thought about it nearly a week."

He feels victorious, but we are just conditioning him.

"Mr. Miller, when you first laid eyes on your wife, how long did it take you to decide this was a girl you'd like to marry?"

If he says anything longer than five minutes he's in trouble!

"We've looked around and we can't find a comparable home for $28,500."

If you get an objection like this, counter it with information about real estate appraising.

"Replacement cost appraising is not used with regard to homes, Mr. Miller. It is used most often in evaluating commercial buildings less than two years old. You would not rebuild your home today exactly the way it was built 11 years ago. Floor plans, building materials, appliances and styles all change rapidly. It usually takes six years before a home buyer breaks even when he sells. What did you pay for this house when you bought it?"

Remembering information given in Chapter 3 that home values in our area appreciate at 2% a year, you can point this out with great effectiveness. The offering price begins to seem more realistic.

Close
the Sale

"Mr. Miller, my time is valuable. Please give me your decision."

Take your time. Be patient but persistent.

"We want to think it over some more. We'll give you our answer tomorrow."

"You know more about this contract right now than you ever will again. Two hours from now you will have forgotten some points. Tomorrow morning you will remember even less. This decision is very important to you both. Make it now, while all the facts are fresh in your minds."

Be persistent. It is a good policy to change the subject completely for a few minutes. Get the sellers' minds off the sale long enough to give them a break. If the sellers are still non-receptive, bring the selling salesman into the conversation. A new personality will be very compelling.

Take your time. Be prepared to spend hours, if need be. Don't ever leave until you have the sellers' signatures on the contract, even if you have to settle for a counter offer.

If the sale is made with government-insured financing, it is the lister's obligation to protect the sellers on the points to be charged.

It may be quite correct that the current point quote on the sale, at the time of the sale, is two points, for example, but points are charged the seller as of the time of the close of escrow. If the point charge declined, the seller would benefit.

But points increase as well as decline. To protect the sellers against this occurrence, write the following legend into the contract just above the space where the sellers sign their names:

Sellers agree to pay a maximum of two FHA (or GI) points.

This not only protects the sellers against an unforeseen rise in points, but it also commits the sellers to pay the necessary points in the first place. In many government-insured contracts, the selling salesman inadvertently omits writing a clause into the contract by which the sellers agree to pay the necessary points.

After the sales contract is signed, keep the sellers informed of the progress of the escrow. To be truly a professional, you must give service.

A Final
Example

With the information recorded on these pages, and an ability to think logically, you can successfully counter any objection posed.

When you are asked questions by homeowners, they want good answers. They don't want evasive, weak, or illogical answers. Think before you speak. The answers will come.

I recently received a telephone call from a gentleman who said he was transferred to another city and had to sell his home. He wanted me to come to his home and discuss the sale with him. I expected an easy listing. How wrong I was!

When I arrived at the home, the owner met me at the door and invited me to take a seat in the living room. He settled himself into a chair opposite me and picked up a paper-laden clipboard and a pen. He was very gracious, but very businesslike.

"Mr. Himmah," he began, "I'm an engineer in the aerospace industry and am transferred all over the country. I've sold five houses and have learned something of the real estate business. In the past, I've picked my broker at random from the phone book but I learned the folly of that.

"I have made a list of eight real estate firms. I selected them from looking at the style of newspaper advertising they use. I have made a list of questions I would like to ask you. I am going to ask the same question of each broker and then I will make my decision as to which firm I will give my listing to."

This was an unorthodox approach, but it was realistic. I thought it might be fun. It was.

"Mr. Himmah, how do you arrive at the listing price of a home? Do you use a square-foot appraisal method?"

It was an excellent question. I was soon to see that all the questions were sound. Every answer was noted on his clipboard.

"Mr. Blake, I don't arrive at a listing price. You do! Let me explain.

"I am not enthusiastic about square-foot appraisals because they don't forecast the emotional reaction a prospective buyer would have to your home. I try to get a feeling about your home and then project myself into the place of the buyer. I weigh my opinion with knowledge I have of sales prices of comparable homes in this neighborhood.

"I do like to get the opinions of several institutional appraisers whose ability I respect."

I then used my standard price discussion, going into the economics of price (i.e. supply, demand, utility).

I showed Mr. Blake I had a good deal of knowledge about the subject of price. We finally arrived at a price, with his help, of course. I later discovered the price I suggested was $1,200 lower than a price another salesman had already given him.

"Mr. Himmah, if I decide to list my home with you, will you advertise it?"

"No!" I answered. "There are three methods of advertising a general brokerage firm can employ. . . ." I went through my standard answer to the advertising question.

"Mr. Himmah, if you were in my position, what would you look for in a real estate firm?"

This question was really loaded. My answer had to be short, to the point, and logical.

"I would look for a firm with a young, aggressive sales force. I would like a larger firm. (After all, I had to describe my own firm! You should prepare a similar story to describe your firm.) I would like the firm to advertise well and liberally. I would want the broker to be actively engaged in the business himself rather than just performing a manager function. I would look for businesslike, professional qualities in the firm. The salesman I spoke to would reflect the professional fiber of the firm. I would want the salesman to be enthusiastic, earnest, and knowledgeable."

Our conversation continued on this format for well over an hour. I must confess that I did not get the listing on that first meeting. The owner was determined to follow his plan. He had been hurt too many times before.

I received a call the following afternoon from Mr. Blake. He told me to come out and write up the listing. I asked him why he decided on my firm.

"I liked your answers," he replied. "Of all the salesmen I talked to, you were the only one who answered all my questions directly, keeping to the point."

The information I gave was known by most salesmen. But most salesmen don't use the information they have at hand.

Study the material on these pages, and think about what you are reading. Amend the various points to fit your own personality and the market conditions in your local area. Listing technique is nothing more than a logical progression of basic selling principles.

That's the story of listing for volume. Study it. Use it. You will be richer for it. I promise you.

Index

B

Bankers as listings sources, 74
Banks:
  commercial, 42
  Federal Reserve System member, 43
  lending capabilities of, 42
  as listings sources, 74
  savings, 42
Briefing the seller, 152–153
Brokerage, significance of listing in, 12
Budget, the advertising, 180
Building and loan associations, 74
Business reports as listings sources, 74
Buyer interest, maintenance of, 125
Buyers:
  burden of points on, 21–22
  emotionalism of, 31
  leads on, 73
  newlyweds as prospective, 72
  posing as a potential, 70–71
  qualification of, 44
  as source of listings, 138
  unknown, 2

C

Canvassing for listings, 71–73
  door to door, 71–72
  by telephone, 72, 79–80
Capabilities, lending:
  bank:
    commercial, 42
    savings, 42

Capabilities, lending (*cont.*)
  insurance company, 41–42
  liquidity factor in, 41
  mortgage company, 42–43
  savings and loan association, 40–41
Cards, listing (*see* Listing cards)
Certificate of Eligibility, VA, 46
Certificate of Reasonable Value, *defined,* 45
Chess, listing likened to, 12–13
Clients (*see* Buyers; Principals; Sellers)
Close, the:
  program of the, 124–127
  timing the, 123–124
Closing the sale, 193–194
  agent's function at, 189–190
  salesman's function at, 189–190
Closing techniques, 123–127
Combat, selling as, 107
Combination listing form, the, 60–61, 66–67
Commercial banks (*see* Banks)
Commission cutting, ethics of, 192
Commission obstacle, the, 108–111
Commission schedules, formulation of, 14
Commissions:
  conditions of payment of, 48
  ethics of, 48, 192
  insuring payment of, 54–55
  listing, 14
  90%, *defined,* 24–25
  sales, 14
  sellers' views of, 90
    countering, 108–111
Communication with sellers, 152–153
Comparative analysis pricing method, the, 32